BRANDING:
The Real Estate Agent

The Complete Guide

To Making It Big In Real Estate

BY
MARK HUGHES
&
AMY YOUNG

Copyright © 2008 Mark Hughes & Amy Young
All rights reserved.

ISBN: 1-4196-9217-8
ISBN-13: 9781419692178

Visit www.booksurge.com to order additional copies.

Contents

Introduction 5
   Mark's Story. 5
Section I The Power of Branding 15
   Chapter 1. Branding and You. 19
      Why Brand? 23
   Chapter 2. Branding 101 27
      Sales 32
Section II Discovering Your Brand 35
   Chapter 3. Self Discovery 39
   Chapter 4. Matching Your Passion
      with Your Niche 47
   Chapter 5. Developing Your Target Market . .53
      Making the Commitment to Specialization. .53
      Exploring Your Niche. 55
Section III Building Your Brand 59
   Chapter 6. Visual Brand Identity 63
      Appearance and Style 63
      Photography 66
      Colors. 70
      Logo. 74
      Tagline 78
      Copywriting 79

  Layout and design....................82
  Standards...........................83
 Chapter 7. Networking...................87
 Chapter 8. Advertising 95
 Chapter 9. Direct Mail Marketing 103
  Just Listed and Just Sold Cards..........106
  Newsletters.........................108
  Niche Specific Postcards...............112
 Chapter 10. Internet Marketing...........115
  Websites...........................115
  Blogging, E-newsletters
   and Social Networking 122
  Search Engines 123
  Email 127
 Chapter 11. Public Relations 131
  Press Releases 133
  Press Kit...........................136
 Chapter 12. Personal Brochure 141
Section IV Being Your Brand................149
 Chapter 13. Branded Systems.............151
 Chapter 14. Brand Standards.............157
  Life Balance 160
 Chapter 15. Brand Testing 163
  Brand Commandments.................165
Conclusion 169
Branding: The Real Estate Agent Workbook ..173
Branded Agent Resources 210
Learn More..............................217
About the Authors 219

Introduction

Mark's story

I grew up as the son of a teacher who worked at a very expensive and exclusive private school in the northeast. I was surrounded by the trappings of wealth all of my growing years. Compared to our neighbors, we had little financially. But I was blessed to grow up with four smart and wonderful older siblings in a beautiful home on the campus. My parents were loving and took great care to instill faith and good values in all of us. We are all still very close and supportive of one another.

Despite my blessed childhood, I grew up wanting all of the things that the other kids at school had. Still, I understood why things were the way they were, and I was a good kid who studied hard. I figured out that I would have to work hard to earn those things that I wanted so badly: toys, clothes, cars, etc. When I discovered branding, I figured out I wouldn't necessarily have to work hard, but I would have to work smart. That's what branding is: working smart. Eventually I would also figure out that life is not about having the "stuff" either; the journey and the relationships along the way are what really matter.

After attending The University of Virginia, I quit the boozy habits, the result of going to college in the 80's, and decided I would try my hand at the many opportunities that real estate offered. A buddy had financed a house with 3% down, slapped some paint on the walls, and flipped the property for thirty thousand in profit. His quick success piqued my interest. Contributing to my eagerness was the fact that I watched him do this while I sat at my desk in a banking job making less than that in a year. So I figured real estate was the place to be.

My path to success in real estate began the moment I realized that I was working in an industry where everyone seemed to be doing the same thing. No one was trying to stand out. As the youngest of five kids, I was used to fighting for attention. As a real estate agent, I felt the same compulsion to get noticed.

As I was growing up, whether for good reasons or bad, I always tried to stand out a bit, to garner a little attention to feed the old ego. What I would realize after years of schooling, both in books and in the ways of people, was that the most rewarding way to stand out was to be authentic. A fake is a fake, and anyone can act a part. But to achieve anything in this world you have to work hard. The law of the farm says you reap what you sow. So I decided to

INTRODUCTION

learn the real estate business, and to set myself apart I would specialize by narrowing my focus to a targeted market.

I took my first licensing class at twenty-two. As I fixed and flipped my own properties I worked in the financing end of the business. I learned, originated, and taught about how to finance real estate. My wife had become an agent in the meantime and was very successful listing and selling homes in and around the area in which we lived. Inherently, she knew the value of specializing and establishing expertise. Farming a particular geographic or demographic niche is nothing new, but how you approach it must be dynamic to make any difference. I realized that listing and selling could be more lucrative for me, so I rolled up my sleeves and started selling real estate in the mid 90's.

I am a numbers guy, and I knew how many people moved in and out of certain areas each year. I knew that if I could be the first agent whom those potential clients thought of, I would make a great living. So I never focused on the technical skills of the business; I just worked on making my name the most recognizable name in the area. I learned the technical skills on the fly, but I promoted my brand right from the start. My business was built on the strength of referrals from satisfied clients. I was able to develop that client base with a brand campaign that exposed consumers to my message through multiple branding channels. My brand identity was a representation of a desirable city lifestyle, and the message was that I was an easygoing and dedicated guy.

I decided to market my services to people who were as passionate about the lifestyle and community as I was. I lived there, raised my family there, worked and played there, and shared happiness and sorrows there. My family became an important part of the community, and the community was part of the fiber of our lives. Tremendous success followed. I employed seven separate channels of marketing and advertising to brand myself as *the* top agent to my audience. Today I call them branding channels, because when I started comparing my technique with those of other top agents, I discovered that these seven focuses were crucial to their success, too. Individually, each channel provides marginal success, but working them simultaneously into a comprehensive seven channel approach dramatically improves market impact.

Many people attempted to copy my brand's look and feel. I was often asked if I had noticed another agent's attempt to copy my ads or website. I didn't mind. In fact, when other agents copied my brand style, I felt validated. Imitation meant that I had created a memorable personal brand in the minds of my target audience, and other agents had taken notice of my success. The fact that my own clients recognized other agents copying my style confirmed that I had created emotional ownership around my

INTRODUCTION

brand. By getting them to buy in and take ownership of my brand, I had achieved invaluable brand equity.

On the personal side, my former loose fraternity lifestyle had left me lacking a true understanding of my own identity. I found myself with a valuable university degree, but also unsure about who I really was. My degree was in modern anthropology, so I had studied the modern human condition, our patterns as humans, and what makes us tick. But to discover my own identity, I dove into the personal help section of the bookstore. I read and listened to everything from Carnegie and Peal, Tony Robbins and Steven Covey, to Wayne Dyer and Deepak Chopra. Through those years I read so much, and spent so much time on self-analysis, that my business coach finally told me that I had read enough and I should just go live! If possible, I recommend a coaching engagement or arrangement to help you spot the things in your business that you may be missing. A reputable business coach can be worth a fortune in business productivity.

I had learned volumes about the human condition. And as far as selling real estate was concerned, it had become clear to me that consumers don't want to be *sold* by people— they want to have *faith* in people. While working hard listing and selling, I tried to find peace, to be grateful, and to spread some happiness wherever I went. I encouraged my wife to let me take over her real estate business so she could spend more time at home with our young children. Everything was going really well. I accumulated the material things I had wanted as a kid, and we had our health and good friends.

In 2000, with some money in our pockets and a mutual love of adventure, Judy, I, and the kids set out to test my branded theories in a new market where we didn't know a soul. I should mention that we also chose a much warmer climate. After a few vacations to Florida, we had fallen in love with the lifestyle that a master planned community could offer both young and old families.

My plan was simple: I would represent the lifestyle that I hoped to market. I created a brand identity that represented my own persona in imagery, colors, copy, logo, tag line, and style. My marketing photo was clean and preppy, and my colors and imagery were a peaceful blue and white accented by wispy palms. My personal comportment was authentic. I was positive, humorous, well prepared, and dedicated. That was my style and brand image, which is branding channel one. I learned to articulate the benefits of the Florida lifestyle. I honestly valued the outdoor, active, warm experience that comes with living there. I was passionate about sharing that kind of life with everyone who was willing to listen.

Next, I began the brand work of networking. I grew my database by a few names every day and actively included new contacts in branded mailings both

INTRODUCTION

online and off. I networked in the athletic club, on the golf course, in neighborhood meetings, and by giving my business card to as many people as I could. I founded, and for the next few years, presided over the most successful business club in my target area. Using my branded image, I consistently ran branded advertising in the targeted but less expensive local newsletters and weekly papers. I mailed out branded postcards, newsletters, and e-newsletters. I consistently sent out press releases on everything that I achieved worth noting. I received more PR from the local press than I could have imagined, just because I tried. Only then did I realize the power of the PR branding channel. The work in public relations proved invaluable, as being a bit famous (or recognizable) is a key element to your brand.

My website was search engine optimized to appear at the top of the list when people were searching in the area or for the lifestyle that I specialized in. In fact, by learning a little about per click advertising and web site optimizing, the website generated enough business that I was able to hire two buyers' agents to help with all the leads. There were enough leads to enable both buyers' agents to individually win area sales volumes awards.

As my team of support staff and agents grew, I made sure not to spoil the brand by promoting the team. People related to me and my brand and wanted the promise and benefit of my expertise, not a delegate, to benefit them and meet their needs. People don't understand working with substitutes, they never will. Assistants are vital, but buyers and sellers want to talk and negotiate with *you*, the face and name they trust. My team rightfully wanted recognition. But as soon as I gave in and ran new "team" ads, I could feel and hear my brand's loss of traction in the market. I backed up and went with the old branding immediately.

Going away from my established brand was almost a disaster. Of course, an agent needs solid administrative support to excel and succeed. I would have never had the success I did without my team. But I've learned that the best team members and assistants are the ones who also understand the importance of the brand. If you treat them with gratitude and respect and compensate them well, they will be priceless additions to your business. They will loyally grow the brand without the need for public recognition. If you don't treat them well, you'll risk the theft of your game plan and the potential threat of their competition. Consistency is paramount, and I've learned that a solid support system that can effectively function as a brand may be difficult to find but essential if you want to succeed.

After putting the seven branding channels into action, I averaged well over half a million dollars a year in real estate income. More importantly, I was able to be the father and husband that I aspired to be. We traveled and visited family often. I worked out daily, grew my faith, and finally got comfortable with my own identity.

SECTION I

The Power of Branding

Real Estate isn't about selling homes, land, or businesses. Like life, real estate is really about personal connections. To make the sale you must present yourself, and your product, in a way that affects your customer on an emotional level. Like running for office or a local committee, real estate sales is about presenting yourself as someone to whom the consumer can relate. How others perceive you will determine if you succeed or fail. So your goal should be to market an image of yourself that will result in a positive outcome.

According to the NAR, 76% of people who decide to list their home with the assistance of a licensed real estate agent interview only one agent for the job. How do you make sure you become that one agent? Thankfully, branding is not about cold calling, learning scripts, practicing closing techniques, or perfecting sales shtick. These things are only fodder for the nearsighted herd, which is what I call the swarms of agents who rely on generic sales tactics.

Branding is also not about file flow systems, software logistics, or database management. Although, all of these real estate essentials can help you grow your personal brand, they should not be your primary focus.

Personal branding in real estate is about discovering, building, and implementing your own personal brand to make you more money and give you more freedom. In today's real estate industry, branding is the only way to succeed. Members of the herd don't get the recognition, referrals, or repeat business needed to make selling real estate a lucrative and fulfilling career.

So how do you stand out from a crowd of agents who offer the same skills, services, and experience that you do? Some agents just seem to stand out. Their experience and skills are not what set them apart, so what does? Their secret is something central to who they are and how they do their business. You can probably picture one or two of these agents right now. What you just imagined was their brand. The image you just recalled, the perception you've created about a particular agent— that's the power of a brand. Why did those specific agents come to mind? Those agents may not be exceptional, but they do have an exceptional image.

Once you master what I call the Seven Channels of personal branding, you can create the life that a high income offers while really enjoying what you do. Neither the skills to create a personal brand nor the actual branding channels are difficult concepts to employ. The difficult part is artfully combining an authentic brand into a consistent and orchestrated branding approach. Most agents understand the value of each individual branding channel, but only branded agents see that their power lies in a comprehensive, ongoing plan to deliver the brand message.

Personal branding not only positions you as the market share leader of your target audience, but it also creates a huge barrier for other agents trying to imitate your strategy. If they do, they actually just help to solidify your branded position by looking like copycats. Branded agents increase their earning potential because recognizable market leaders can maintain higher commissions when decisions become less about the money and more about perceived familiarity and expertise.

Most significantly, a good personal brand will bring balance back into the life of a hectic real estate agent. By creating focus and limiting your targets, you will create more business with increased market share and stature. Your brand will free up the time you need for family, health, and spirit because your campaign will continue to work for you even when you aren't available. Time management instills balance into your life and helps you to become even better at what you do. Branding gives you the income and confidence to nurture the family, health, and recreation in your life.

A good personal brand can bring you peace of mind, financial comfort, and help you maintain passion for what you do. You have chosen real estate as your calling; now you must strive to achieve your maximum potential. I've heard business leaders say, "Find what you love to do, and the money will follow." I can gladly say that I have found that to be true, and I want to show you how you too can be successful doing what you love.

The great news is that everyone is brand-worthy. Everyone has distinct personal qualities, unique selling propositions, and other individual offerings that bring something exclusive to your brand. You are about to take on a task that members of the herd refuse to attempt. You are going to create and market your own brand.

Chapter 1

Branding and You

So how do you unearth your unique promise of value and then deliver that message to your target market? How do you become the one agent that prospects think of first when buying and selling? The following three simple concepts are what you will need to develop your own personal brand. Through this process of **discovering, building,** and **implementing** your brand, you will take a close look at your authentic self to discover the brand that you were always meant to be. In doing so, you'll create a rejuvenating career path based on a clear specialization that you enjoy. If done correctly, your persona as a successful realtor will be an extension of your authentic self, allowing you to thoroughly enjoy what you do *and* be successful.

Once you discover the brand that best suits you as an individual, you will learn to build that brand from the ground up. Through this process you will be in control of guiding the public perception of you as a professional. There are several components that make up this step, but if you commit to putting your time and energy into them, you will be rewarded immensely. Like Cartier, Coach, or Starbucks, you too can be sought after and perceived as the brand of choice if you work diligently during this stage of the game.

Finally, through implementation you will learn the value of consistency as you are guided through the actual steps needed to become and maintain your individual brand. Your commitment and drive will propel your business forward, and you will begin to see the benefits of your hard work. And although branding is a long term process, you will be surprised by how quickly you will experience the abundant rewards of branding.

An entire brand identity consists of relevant and consistent imagery, colors, copy, logos, and tag lines. With an authentic style and brand image established, you can more effectively utilize advertising, direct mail, networking, personal brochures, the Web, and other advertising. A consistent, multi-media campaign will establish a clear identity for your brand and shape your audience's perception.

Creators of the world's most successful brands know that an effective brand is synonymous with a solid reputation. Nike, Michael Jordan, Haagan Daaz, Starbucks, Google, BMW, Martha Stewart…your shirt, your shoes, your ice cream, your coffee, your search engine, your car, and your style are all products of successful branding. Nike buyers perceive that they can achieve their personal best with Nike rather than another shoe. Some athletes believe they can better quench their thirst with Gatorade over other sport drinks. Safety minded drivers prefer Volvos for safety and security over other automobile options. Disney is the preferred family entertainment provider for millions over other family get-away choices. Starbucks is much more than coffee; the company is a consistent brand experience of product, design, and service.

Successful companies understand the power of a brand and use branding to market everything from socks to diamond rings. When consumers see the Tiffany blue box, they don't just think of jewelry. They see a box that represents quality, taste, classic styling, and luxury—something that a man would be proud to give his wife–a sure thing. But Tiffany didn't establish such a reputation with just a little blue box. The public perception of the company was created through expansive ad campaigns, quality in-store experiences, consistent product quality, distinctive style, and luxurious images. Powerful public identities do not happen over night, but with the help of a carefully designed brand, they can be developed.

The big-brand companies have researched the branding phenomenon for years and found several benefits. For example, most consumers are willing to pay an additional 5–7% more for a brand that they recognize and trust. Consider the Starbucks $4 cup of coffee, which so many consumers choose over the $1 convenience store version. You wouldn't walk into an unfamiliar coffee shop in a new town and pay $4 for a coffee when you can't be guaranteed the product will meet your expectations. But thanks to powerful branding, you are quite happy to pay a premium price for coffee in any Starbucks in the world. You believe that the product you purchase will be exactly what you expect because you've experienced the brand before. The consistent imagery, atmosphere, colors, logo, employees, and other branded messages are all there to reinforce your expectations.

Similarly, chances are that when you hear the names Oprah, Michael Jordan, Donald Trump, or Tiger Woods, you immediately know who they are and what they represent. They have truly mastered the power of personal branding. At the mention of their names you call to mind images of their faces, their products, their slogans, and their areas of expertise. You might even feel like you know them, or at least can relate to them enough that you rely on their personal endorsement of products. If Oprah says, "I loved this book—everyone should read it," that book becomes a bestseller over night.

The ability of celebrities to influence consumers developed from powerful and consistent branding campaigns. This is the ultimate goal for any marketer. As companies and individuals build powerful, influential personal brands, they virtually marginalize non-branded competition. They can only be stopped if they fail to deliver on the promises established in the brand message. In other words, their power is only limited by their own discipline.

Why Brand?

Branding can be defined as making an indelible mark or impression on someone. In real estate, branding influences perception and communicates value to a target group of potential clients. The ultimate goal of branding is to build immediate association; you want your name to be the first that comes to mind. Twenty percent of real estate agents do 80% of the business. What do those twenty percent have in common? They are branded. They are unique, specialized, consistent, and they are the first agents that their target audience remembers. Branded agents are the ones that stand out from the herd. They are able to break through the crowd of agents and set themselves apart as unique and effective.

How are they able to break free from the herd? They combine several different marketing channels to create and present a positive image to their target markets. Because they specialize in particular niches, branded agents understand better than anyone else the wants and need of their clients. They become experts in specific areas and work to continuously promote a consistent brand message. In short, expertise and consistent brand exposure help them to maintain elevated brand positioning over the rest of the herd.

A brand also tells customers what they can expect from an agent. In today's world people generally don't care who you are unless you show them why they should. Personal branding is the process of combining your skills, personality, and unique characteristics into a powerful identity that sets you apart from your competitors. A good personal brand will evoke positive images and feelings in consumers. Branding allows agents to enjoy longevity, fulfillment, premiums, and wealth in an industry where statistically the majority of licensees don't last two years. Branding doesn't replace hard work, planning, or performance, but a good brand is virtually impossible to compete against.

The process of discovering and building your brand has to happen before you begin marketing or selling. You need to discover what makes you different, what qualities you have that benefit your target market, and how you can consistently deliver your brand message. Agents are wasting their time if they begin advertising without first developing a personal brand.

In the herd your business depends entirely on your personal involvement. You have to hunt down new clients, place ads, design marketing pieces, show homes, and service listing clients. You spend long days that may result in high profits one month, only to find yourself scrambling to make your mortgage the next. Once you employ an authentic personal brand, you can stop chasing sales. Business will start to come to you.

Your personal brand works as a proxy for you with prospects and potential clients. By continuously representing you even in your absence, a personal brand consistently presents a positive image to your target audience. Your brand tells consumers how you are different, why you are relevant, and puts you at the top of the list.

Branding separates the best from the rest. Through consistent brand exposure an agent's message works its way into consumers' memory banks. As they make decisions, your brand immediately pops up as a logical choice. Instead of selling a product, a brand gives people the information they need to sell themselves on the product. Brands are unique promises of value.

Simply put: Effective Branding = Unlimited Power. Branding gives you the power to shape the public's perception of who you are and what you stand for, along with establishing why you are worthy of their business. If done well, your product or name can become the brand of choice, the expert, and the authority in your area of specialization. Branding is the surest way to gain explosive income growth, respect from your peers and clients, and longevity in your career.

Through branding, you become the one that your clients trust, the one they refer to their friends, the one with which they want to associate, and the one they buy from again and again. When you're branded well, you have more time, you enjoy your career more, and success comes much more easily to you. Most importantly, by building your brand from an authentic foundation, you don't have to worry about pretending to be someone that you're not. The best way to success is to brand your unique self, quirks and all. You'll be genuine, sincere, and relatable. Your clients will connect with your authenticity and credibility. It's simple, people do business with those whom they like, and most people like honest, real individuals.

Chapter 2

Branding 101

The History of Branding

To understand your potential Branding power you must first understand the psychology and history of Brands. Branding originally started with tangible products from companies like DuPont, which became a reliable household name. Brands were products that were dependable, readily available, and affordable. Sears Roebuck, for example, became a dependable brand because of a vast product line of relevant goods delivered conveniently and efficiently to customers around the country. Perhaps contributing even more to Sears success was the visual style and identity that was consistently presented through the Sears catalog. People loved the catalog because the images inside represented a brighter world, a better life, and solutions to life's daily demands.

Commonly lumped with marketing, branding is actually a very different concept. Marketing is a quick active message designed to sell a product. Branding is the slow process of building, over time, a recognizable image. While marketing consists of all the things you do to get your product or service in front of the consumer, branding consists of the things you do to shape the *perception* of that product or service. Over time branding will actually reduce costly unfocused marketing campaigns by targeting a specific market with a collaborative seven channel branding approach.

So many companies are vying for people's attention every day. Most shotgun marketing campaigns attempt to catch anyone that may need a product at a particular moment. Often, particularly in real estate, there is no thought to a concerted brand approach. Instead, agents advertise sporadically. Without a branding approach most agent marketing and advertising campaigns are a total waste of money. Traditional advertising might bring in a deal but will not lay the groundwork for long-term recognition or credibility.

The average person is bombarded by over three thousand brand impressions a day. Three thousand brand impressions a day! All of that stimulus has got to be tiresome. People are no doubt exhausted by the advertisement-saturated media. In fact, consumers are so fed up with the marketing invasion, they have rightfully created their own no spin zones. The presence of advertising and marketing everywhere has created generations of dismissive and jaded consumers. Consumers have had enough. They have been sold to and have been continually pressured to the point that they are just plain skeptical of all salespeople.

Some advertisements make bigger impressions than others, but the impressions that have lasting impact are *branded* products or services that have leveraged multiple channels of exposure and have proven to be unique, relevant, and consistent. Each exposure increases the perception that the product and message are still working, available, and beneficial. Thus, over time, a brand strongly encourages consumer decisions. A successful brand does not get consumers' attention by ramming ideas down their throats, but by exposing them repeatedly to a message that directly addresses the needs, expectations and interests of the target market. Each branding channel is validated and supported by the same consistent brand exposures through other channels. Branded newsletters add to similarly branded Internet ads, which reinforce the magazine ads, etc. All present the same message.

Branding is not something you'll learn in licensing class or at the office. Brokerages have traditionally held on to as much brand power as possible. Historically, managers have been careful not to give up too much power or to encourage agents to brand themselves, as they saw this as a detriment to the company. Managers didn't promote individual brands because that would have shifted the focus from the company to the agent, giving the agent too much influence and recognition. Manager's also knew that if the company brand was bringing in the sales then more new agents would join the office and bring more business. But shouldn't the agent have the power? After all, the agent does the work that makes the company successful.

Managers feared that agents could be more memorable than the company, which would hurt the company's vital necessity of recruiting new agents. They were also afraid that the agent, once becoming more recognizable than the company brand, would leave to start a new business. So traditionally owners and brokers chose to promote the company brand and play down the individual agent brand.

Without a handle on branding, managers have resorted to sale incentive programs, which lift up a few top agents but actually demoralize the majority of others. Managers promote direct mail, web marketing, advertising, and networking, but their tutelage lacks other key branding components. Very little guidance other than "go get 'em," "don't forget to farm," and "send out those just sold cards" has been given to new agents. The problem is that an agent can't just send out a direct mail piece or advertise in one magazine and expect to see results.

Typically, most people can remember only about two top agents. And they are always branded agents. If you ask the same people what company these agents work for, most of the time, they aren't quite sure. People usually do business with agents who have branded themselves as likable, believable, and trustworthy, regardless of the company they represent. The branded agent trumps the company brand almost all of the time.

Finally, companies, owners, and managers are starting to understand the tremendous effects of playing a supporting role in the personal brand of their best agents. The owners are choosing to protect the company brand and let the agent bring in the profit by creating a great personal brand. They are beginning to see the increased value of personal branding as a tool to gain market share and provide longevity for their agents. Through resources and support, real estate companies are beginning to help agents find their own brands.

Also, branded agents understand they don't necessarily make more money by starting their own real estate companies; they make money by maintaining personal brand presence and putting together real estate deals. Agents with the best personal branding have always called their own shots, and more and more they are now able to do so comfortably under the umbrella of the parent company.

Sales

The biggest misconception that the herd of agents has about there own business is that they are primarily in the business of selling homes. Branded agents know that they are really in the business of marketing themselves and selling homes along the way. Branding is about working smarter, not necessarily harder. Selling is convincing. No matter what commissioned salespeople are selling, they usually have to work for every cent. Sales is a brutal business. Selling is tough and exhausting, so naturally you want to get the bulk of your business through more efficient avenues.

Selling is the act of creating a need where one does not exist. You chase customers who don't want to listen, and then you try to make them listen. For most, sales is wrestling for dollars, with no thought of the customer's emotional needs. Selling is alienating. For years, sales training has been focused on teaching manipulative techniques that actually damage or destroy the relationship. Consumers have caught on and don't want to be *sold to* anymore; they want to be in control.

Most people love to buy; they just don't like being pressured into it. So how you close the sale is not as important as building a trusting relationship. By taking the few seconds you are given with each branding impression, you can set the perception that you are the one to solve customers' problems and meet their needs. Consumers want their needs put first, and your brand needs to keep reinforcing a promise to do just that.

Today more than ever, consumers buy with their hearts as much as with their heads. Instead of focusing on sales skills, work on channeling your brand message to the right audience. Let people become familiar with your business. The goal is to get people to like you, trust you, and believe you. A strong personal brand does the heavy lifting by getting you past sales resistance. Branded agents work less, have a higher return on marketing investment, and close more deals than the herd.

The Real Estate business is changing. Sadly, our profession doesn't have the most positive or admired reputation. With only limited guidelines for entry, the Real Estate industry is exposed to many part-timers, hobbyists, and inexperienced investors looking to earn a quick buck. We are often viewed as selfish, shrewd salespeople that will do just about anything to make money. For example, some agents promote themselves with proclamations like, "Multi-million dollar producer." This has only added to our profession's negative image, because the average consumer assumes we make millions while doing very little work. That kind of marketing doesn't exactly inspire them to help us add to our perceived wealth. Through Branding, you have the opportunity to distinguish yourself from the negative perception that Real Estate agents have by guiding the perception of your personal brand identity. If done well, you will be recognized as one of the few professional "good ones," which will lead to new levels of growth in your business.

Branding allows you to pre-sell yourself with a targeted and relevant message that conveys the right information about you, your values, and your position. Being pre-sold through your branding provides an enormous advantage over everyone else that has to find a way to build credibility with their potential clients. Branding eliminates the need for the hard sell and the pushy salesman approach. Times have changed and you need to adapt as well.

Branding allows your consumers to pat themselves emotionally on the back for finding you, their favorite brand. And you are marketing your image to them in a gentle way that is so unobtrusive, they think they developed that perception all by themselves. When people choose you as their brand of choice because of the relevant benefits implied by your consistent brand message, you will encounter very little sales resistance. The herd must attend the same tired sales seminars and learn tedious scripts and closing techniques to convince new consumers to buy. The herds approach is outdated and intrusive. People choose your brand because they feel you understand them.

SECTION II

Discovering Your Brand

Qualifying as a good agent these days comes down to one thing–perception. Consumers often don't investigate any further than what they've been told, experienced, or personally witnessed. They trust only what they see and hear. And, if you've branded yourself well, the right clients are hearing and seeing exactly what you want them to.

Consumers accept branding and the agents who use a brand to their advantage. Potential clients trust what they have seen and heard and don't even think of asking branded agents the tough questions: How long have you been in business? Or, would you consider reducing your commission? The agent's branding speaks for itself. A brand tells consumers all that they need to know – the agent is respected, proven, and an all-around good person.

With that said, guess what potential clients are seeing and hearing about *you*? If you are like most agents, you haven't established a brand, so consumers have heard nothing. Most have probably never heard your name and don't even realize that you're an agent. If this is the case, you'll never make the cut. You can't even begin to compete with the branded agent, even though he may not have near the amount of skill or experience that you do. Are you going to let these agents simply step in and take over your hard earned market share?

The time has come to fight back. Find your niche and live it, breathe it, and promote it. Word of mouth can be your best publicity. Creating the kind of buzz that gets you noticed really isn't that difficult, but it is very necessary to make sure you make your business the success you deserve. The ball is in your court. Make a name for yourself *today* so you can start to enjoy all the flexibility and prosperity that comes along with agent stardom. Or you can simply continue with your current approach and the life that you've been living. This is your choice, but just remember: great results require action.

Real Estate is a challenging industry, especially for those looking to excel. There is infinite competition, little training, and no guarantee of success. On the upside, however, our industry offers unlimited opportunity to make the kind of money about which most people only dream. What's even better is that once you master the secrets of this business, you can have it all – the life, the prosperity, the flexibility, the family time. But everything is really all up to you, not potential clients, or your company, but you.

Your brand identity is a powerful way for the world to see and value the authentic you. Be true to your own personality, spirit, and character. Where relationships are concerned, authenticity is what people want most. You can't fake this aspect of your business. You don't have to share all of the same values with every client, but you do need to be able to honestly relate to them. If you feel like a phony because you don't have a brand and you don't know what makes you unique or relevant, you are not alone. Stay confident about your brand creation because the idea is uniquely yours and, as such, will never become a commodity. Creating a brand is also a great opportunity to reevaluate yourself and discover or confirm your true identity. Getting your spirit aligned with your business and presenting yourself authentically is the right step.

The secrets to success in real estate aren't really secrets at all but are organic and simple branding concepts that have been around for ages. You have to become a Brand, but not just any brand. You must become the most authentic and relevant brand that you can possibly be. By looking inside to discover your true self, matching your passion with a niche market that will respond to you, making the commitment to specialize your business, and exploring your new niche to truly understand your targeted customers better, you will be on your way to discovering the brand that represents you perfectly. This is the brand that your competition will envy, the one that will resonate with your customers, and the one that will ultimately bring you to super star agent status if you so choose.

Chapter 3

Self Discovery

When trying to earn respect and trust from anyone today, authenticity is the standard by which we are all judged. Self analysis will allow you to create a brand that will anchor and improve your relationship with your target market. When you are authentic, you strike a chord with people. Consumers value your passion and begin to identify with your efforts. Since you've chosen a niche you truly love, your target market will recognize your sincerity and put their trust in you.

By taking the time to thoroughly analyze yourself, your interests and your passions, you will begin to separate yourself from the endless sea of competing agents. Most realtors don't take the time to develop a solid foundation and usually do not understand the importance of self-analysis. That's ok; let them continue to chase their next deal. Let them worry about how they are going to make their next mortgage payment. You just keep working to find your own passion. Find something that you truly enjoy and that you would love to include in the rest of your life. Today's agents can no longer effectively differentiate ourselves touting superior service, more knowledge, or better products, but we can stand out for who we are and how we translate that into what we do. We are the product. We are the only thing that is different in this business, and we need to use that asset to our advantage.

Personal Branding is not about building your ego or bragging. A brand is simply the way to present the best you. The 'You' that is relevant and valued by your family, peers, and customer base. When you're trying to discover yourself and your brand, concentrate on being true, rather than trying to please everyone. There will be some consumers who do not respond positively to your brand, but keep your focus on the ones who will. Remember you are specializing and marketing yourself to a specific group. The rest of the population will not impact your business, and that's just fine. You must not try to be someone who you're not. Most people are skeptical and tired of phony personas and promises. If they decide to work with you, they have expectations, and they don't want to be let down.

Begin today by looking at yourself differently. You are a brand. You may not be aware that you already have a personal brand making an impression on the public. Your consumers already have a perception of you. If you don't know what their perception is, then you need to take back the control. As you begin developing your personal brand, keep in mind that you are laying the foundation that will carry you through your career. Do not breeze through this process. The goal is to find a brand that you are naturally comfortable with day in and day out. Start by defining who you are, what you stand for, and how you'd like to be perceived. Take your time and put some serious thought into this.

Brainstorming the following questions will help you better understand your personal passions, qualities, skills, and values. Set aside some time so you can focus on answering these questions thoughtfully. Your answers may surprise you, but they will give you clear insight into your authentic self. For further inspiration, have friends, family members, and colleagues answer the same questions as if they were you. Their answers will reveal the kind of impression that you make on others. If your answers have obvious differences, then the brand that you are currently projecting isn't authentic and will need some work.

Your passions
1. *What are you passionate about?*
2. *What would you do every day if you didn't need to work?*
3. *If you could only pick one activity to do for the rest of your life what would it be?*

Your qualities
4. *What is unique about you?*
5. *What is your most distinct personal characteristic?*
6. *What do you get most compliments on?*

Your skills
7. What is your greatest strength?
8. What is unique about your services?
9. What do you do that adds a distinctive value?

Your values
10. What do you value most in life?
11. What are you most proud of?
12. What do you want to be known for?

Gather all of your feedback and review the answers for questions *1–3*. If you've answered honestly, you should notice an underlying theme in your answers. This is what you truly enjoy. Now consider those answers; how can you combine what you love with what you do for a living? There is a good chance that others are passionate about the same things. Start researching the organizations and groups that are associated with your favorite activities and interests. Where do the members of these groups live, work, and play? What other things do they enjoy? As you begin to investigate the people and places associated with your passion, you begin to discover the perfect target market.

Did your friends and colleagues come up with similar answers about your interests? If not, you may be keeping the things you love to yourself. A personal brand cannot hide the things you care about; a clear passion about something is needed for the brand to succeed. Before, you may have thought that work and personal interests should be kept separate. The beauty of authentic personal branding is that you are obligated to create an atmosphere where your work *relies* on the things you are passionate about, allowing you to take pleasure in what you do every day.

Your answers to questions 4–6 will help you identify your unique qualities. These are the mannerisms, characteristics, and quirks that define you as an individual. Finding a place for your unique attributes in your brand is important as they are critical to your authenticity and appeal. If you are lucky enough to have a truly distinguishing quality, take advantage of the opportunity. Agents have been very successful carving out niches based on unique qualities such as being extraordinarily tall, a twin, or from a specific area. Remember, most people enjoy working with agents that they can relate to, so your brand should include your unusual attribute. If you do not have something drastically unique, your lesser distinctive traits will be just as useful in positioning your brand.

We are very familiar with ourselves, so knowing which personal attributes resonate with others can be difficult to determine on our own. Look closely at how your friends and colleagues answered these questions. Their feedback may shed light on additional qualities that you have overlooked. If one answer consistently appears, make note. That trait is distinguishable to friends and family for a reason, and that is the type of quality you want to focus on when defining your brand.

The purpose of questions 7–9 is to determine your skills and strengths. These questions will direct you more towards your professional style, but they can also relate to life in general. In addition to your answers and the feedback from your peers, also jot down any praise or comments that you consistently receive from satisfied clients, managers, and coworkers. If you have the foresight to send out evaluations to your customers, now is a good time to review their comments as well. The information that you gather from all of these sources will help you to pinpoint your best skills, the services your clients most appreciate, and the unique value proposition that ultimately differentiates you from the herd.

Acknowledge underlying themes within the information you gather. Evaluating your own skills is difficult, as you may consider your extraordinary services to be standard procedures. If something is noted by friends and former customers, make sure to add their comments to your list. The whole purpose for his exercise is to help you recognize what matters to your client base. These skills make you different and will enhance your brand. They need to be highlighted when you work on defining your brand.

The final set of questions is also the most important. The way you answer these questions will be very revealing. These are your values and the most significant parts of your life. The reason that you work so hard day in and day out, and the reason you are trying to better yourself right now is so you have more time to focus on these very things. Your values represent who you are at the core, and they will be the nucleus of your personal brand.

You may be interested in the way your friends and peers responded to these final questions as well. Their opinions will give you an idea of how honest you have been in portraying your current brand identity. Ultimately, you are the only person who can answer these specific questions. Your answers are what matter most, as you are the only one who can express your values. If your values don't match what your peers believed of you, then you haven't done a good job of expressing the focus of your authentic brand. That's okay. The purpose of this exercise is to discover your true self and resolve any discrepancies between what you think you are presenting and what you actually *are* presenting.

Next you need to compile all of data you've collected. This exercise should have been an eye opening experience for you. Feel free to pat yourself on the back. By doing this introspective work you've already outpaced most of your competition. Most agents don't take the time to really figure out what they enjoy, what skills they possess, and what unique qualities set them apart. By doing this work upfront you are one step closer to building the brand that will easily bring you more clients, more enjoyment, and more money.

Chapter 4

Matching Your Passion with Your Niche

If you put good thought into the questions in the previous section and noted your results, then you've completed all of the hard work required to find the best suited niche for you and your brand. Next you must make sense of the research that you've gathered. If you were honest with yourself during the exercise and accepted the constructive feedback of your peers, then you have in front of you your very own passions, qualities, skills, and values. Use this information to devise the perfect niche for you.

For help in determining a successful target market, there are four measures that will keep you on track. By acknowledging your passions, pinpointing your unique focus, matching your image with your marketplace, and analyzing your target's potential, you will be able to determine the niche that will support your long term career goals.

First, look specifically at your passions: what among your passions speaks to you the most? This is the best place to find your niche. Many agents make the mistake of thinking that a niche should be completely unique. In actuality, your niche should stem from a larger, common idea. By definition a niche is a position, preferably one that is underserved, that someone can make their own. Your focused position on this larger idea is what will make you unique and allow you to own your chosen niche.

The second step is to narrow your focus to form a niche that you can easily and authentically make your own. For example, luxury homes are a common segment in real estate, but you'll need to dial in further to pinpoint a niche within the luxury market that is right for you. When you think of your big picture passion, ask yourself what you *specifically* like.

In the luxury home example, an agent may be particularly fond of a quaint, high end, lake front community where he had spent some time vacationing. The agent may experience real enjoyment when strolling on the boardwalk in this community and may love spending hours shopping and experiencing the local culture in the village. This community would make a perfect niche for this agent. He already enjoys the environment and has a desire to learn more about the location and the people who live there.

MATCHING YOUR PASSION WITH YOUR NICHE

You may also find your niche during other parts of your self analysis. As I mentioned before, any unique trait can spark a niche. The best niches, however, stem from passion, so make sure that your unique skill or characteristic is something that you are proud of if you'd like to explore it as a niche. For example, since most people are proud of where they came from, your unique heritage could offer opportunities for an effective niche. But if you are an identical twin who thrives on independence and can't stand the constant attention of being an identical twin, then that unique trait will not make the best niche for you.

Now that you have a good grasp of the niche that you are developing, ask yourself, "Do I fit in?" The third step in developing your niche is to determine whether or not you are a good match for the marketplace that you have chosen. The people who live, work, and play within this niche will be the same people with whom you will be interacting daily. The more you naturally match up with them, the more you will enjoy your career and prosper. If you have chosen the right niche, you'll discover that you fit in perfectly. You'll find that your relationships, clients, and referrals will come easier as the potential clients within your niche will feel comfortable working with someone who shares their same interests.

When you don't naturally "fit in" a niche, long term success is much more difficult to attain. You will end up feeling like a phony and will have to work harder trying to create a false impression. This is exhausting and a sure way to lead to burn out. You will end up much more fulfilled if you align with your niche and fit in naturally.

The final step in discovering your niche is to financially analyze your target market. After all, to be successful your niche has to be large enough to support your income goals. You'll need some basic local information to get started: the average turnover for your area and your goal in terms of annual transactions. If you do not know the turnover percentage for your area, simply ask your broker or local board of realtors for the information. The more specific the information, the more accurate your results will be. With this in mind, if your niche is a geographical area, your local title company or tax roll system can assist you in providing more accurate percentages for your specific target market.

When determining your goals, you should take into account the average sales price within your niche. You will need that information to determine the total number of annual transactions that you will need to support your goal. For example, let's say the average home price in Niche A is $300,000. Assuming a 3% co-broke commission, the average commission in Niche A is $9,000. Agent A's annual income goal is $200,000. To reach this income goal,

Agent A must sell 22.2 homes annually. The formula is as follows:

1. Average Home Price × Average Commission = Average Commission
   $300,000 × 3% = $9000

2. Income Goal ÷ Average Commission = Transaction Goal
   $200,000 ÷ $9000 = 22.2 Homes

This formula doesn't account for any brokerage splits, but you can figure in your split by taking the average commission and multiplying that by your share.

Once you have set your goals and determined the annual turnover rate for your area, you can easily verify whether or not your niche is large enough for you to reach your goals. To do this, begin by doubling your transaction goal. Assuming you need to sell 22.2 homes a year, you will want your market to support at least 44.4 homes per year. Doubling the number accounts for the fact that you will still have competing realtors in your market area who will also sell some of the inventory. If you base your analysis simply on your own goals, you will have to sell every home within your niche to be successful, which adds a lot of unnecessary pressure and is virtually impossible. Instead, inflate your goal to allow for competition and divide your doubled goal by your turnover percentage to determine the minimum number of homes needed for your niche to be successful. The formula following assumes a turnover rate of 4%:

2 × Transaction Goal ÷ Turnover Rate = Minimum # of Homes per Niche

1. 2 × 22.2 = 44.4
2. 44.4 ÷ .04 = 1,110 Homes

In this example, the agent's success will rely on a niche that includes at least 1,110 homes. Use these simple formulas to analyze your niche market. If you determine that your niche is too small to sustain your goals, you may need to broaden your focus a bit more, or add a secondary authentic niche. Once you have decided on the niche that is the right size for your income goals, you will be set up for success.

Chapter 5

Developing Your Target Market

Making the Commitment to Specialization

Part of developing your niche is making a commitment to specialization. As a Realtor you are equipped with the same inventory as the next guy. You cannot hang your hat on having the premium product or the best price. Your product and pricing are exactly the same as those of the other thousands of Realtors that you are competing against. Your industry knowledge and skill sets are most likely fairly similar as well. So why do only a few agents reach star status in this reasonably even playing field, while the majority fumble through their real estate careers waiting desperately for their next deal?

A common belief in advertising is that specialization implies expertise. This idea is especially applicable in real estate, where the super agents have mastered specialization. Just as the medical field has cardiologists, neurologists, and thoracic surgeons, the real estate industry has agents that focus on Lakefront properties, corporate businesses, or a specific lifestyle. Specialization implies that you have such a high level of knowledge about a particular field that you are able to handle every detail. This is your specialty? Then you must be an expert. Experts have answers and are immediately credible. As a result, consumers are drawn to experts and are willing to pay a higher fee for their services.

In Real Estate credibility can be difficult to gain right out of the gate, but with effective branding of your specialization you will reach potential clients and begin to form personal relationships with them before you ever meet. As more agents understand the value in specializing, they will see the advantage of sharing information and giving out referrals. As each carves out a personal niche, agents will no longer feel that everyone is chasing the same client. Specialization creates the agent synergy that managers have been trying but failing to foster for decades.

With all of the noted benefits of specializing, this still seems to be one of the steps to which agents have the hardest time committing. Agents are afraid of pigeonholing their business. Many believe that if they miss out on opportunities that don't fall within their niche, they won't be able to grow. This fear, however, is very damaging, as you can never truly specialize if you still experiment in a little bit of everything. The adage "Jack of all trades, master of none" rings very true. The reality is that by tightening your focus, you dramatically strengthen your appeal, but when you become a generalist, you lose that appeal. Would you go to your family physician for plastic surgery? Would you trust a cardiologist to deliver your baby? Of course not. Like any other patient, you would seek a specialist. Failure to develop a specialty lumps you with the herd, where you will never reach your maximum potential.

Exploring Your Niche

Now that you have chosen the perfect niche and made the commitment to specialize, the time has come for some exploration. By learning more about your niche than anyone else, you will be in the perfect position to begin building your brand. Consider this crucial step the market research for your company. With the information you gather, you'll best position yourself to become the market leader. Besides becoming an expert on your niche, you will also learn exactly where to advertise and what will evoke the biggest response from your audience. This kind of insider knowledge will save you thousands in wasted marketing costs. Believe me, very few realtors take the time to do any kind of research. Your niche research will become your secret weapon.

To get to know your niche, begin by immersing yourself in the community. Talk to people, join community groups, and set up lunches with community members and leaders that may influence your niche. Get to know the "hot points," or the issues that make a difference to your niche residents. Most importantly, after any conversation, take a minute in your car or office to recap what you've learned. Compile the information in your database or journal. The information that you gather will become a great resource to you throughout your career. You will be amazed by how many leads you can generate when you just take the time to listen.

Secondly, research your niche by reading. Subscribe to any local or trade periodicals that are specific to your niche. Newspapers and magazines will provide great insight on hot topics and community trends. You'll also get a sense of what is important to your audience. Publishers want to sell more papers, so they are in tune with the topics that are important to your niche. Newspapers and magazines that are specific to your niche have the same target market as you, so they are a good resource in determining the issues and activities that matter to your niche.

In addition to local publications, research all of the basic niche demographic numbers and trends you can get your hands on. If your niche is based on a geographical area, you can easily find demographic information that will be very useful on the web, or in community government offices. If not, you may be able to get similar information from niche specific directories, club lists, and by joining those organizations within your niche. Again, add what you find to your accumulated research so you can easily refer to the information at any time.

The third method of research is to simply take the time to observe. Frequent your niche's market area if you do not already. Have lunch within the community, visit gathering opportunities with your family, and attend events that are niche-related. And *pay attention.* Please don't confuse observing with stalking or spying. Simply take a moment to recognize the activities that are taking place. What type of lifestyle are these people living and aspiring to? Do they seem to be active or reserved, fashionable or careless, outgoing or private, formal or casual? How do they interact with other community members, and how often? In general, are they vocal, proud, or reserved? Are they hard working, or do they value down time? All of the traits that you notice will help you to understand your chosen target market better, so again, be sure to document your findings in your journal.

Review everything that you've learned and categorize the data as much as possible.

This process is almost like creating a blueprint of your target niche. Examples of commonalities to include are:

- Likes and dislikes
- Important local issues
- Activities

- Style
- Preferred recreation
- Preferred schools and colleges
- Local hotspots
- Organizations
- Popular events
- Publications
- Qualities
- Skills
- Values

Finally, once your notebook is full of information about your niche, compare the findings with what you've learned about your own qualities, skills, and values. Refer back to the self analysis exercise you completed earlier in this section and look for similarities. Do you have any shared qualities, skills, or values with the people in your niche? If so, those characteristics will be extremely effective in positioning your brand within your niche.

You have discovered the perfect niche for yourself and have done all of the preparation to ensure a solid foundation. You are the perfect fit for your clients and the obvious agent to help with their real estate needs. Now you have to make your move. Your next step is to create an authentic brand based on the niche that you have just discovered and explored.

SECTION III

Building Your Brand

Now that you've discovered the personal brand that best fits your personality, interests, values, and goals you can start to build your real estate career. There are seven channels to a comprehensive and proven personal branding approach to real estate sales. Each piece is individually important to your business, but implemented together they powerfully enforce your position as a truly branded agent.

Most agents still don't understand what is necessary to really succeed as a realtor today.

Everyone in the herd claims to provide the best customer service, sell the most homes, or be the best marketer. Being the "best" no longer matters that much to consumers. Being the "best" no longer separates you from the herd. Consumers are inundated with agent promotions full of tired superlatives and unsubstantiated claims. Unfortunately for all of us, consumers have decided that all realtors are the cookie-cutter, self-aggrandizing home pushers that make too much money. People are tired of hearing that we made a few million dollars or reached the unfathomable "platinum" club for the third straight year. Consumers don't care about our boasting. And bragging actually sends the wrong message.

But the herd keeps bragging their way to mediocrity, which is really all that a multi-million dollar producer and a platinum club member amounts to. Your goal is to reach people on an emotional level. People need to like you, believe you can help, and trust that you will. The extent to which your brand answers those three concerns will determine the level of real estate success you will achieve.

No one in the herd ever achieves much more than mediocrity. Sure, there may be safety in numbers, but there certainly aren't riches. The herd doesn't take risks, and as a result they get very little reward. Unfortunately for them, continuing to use the same ridiculous real estate marketing methods will continue to produce the same lackluster results. You've seen what I'm talking about: the agent mug shot with a property picture, three lines of description and the tagline, "Sally Sells" in the Saturday paper. This advertising method is not a recipe for longevity or significant success in real estate. But the ad runs every week. The majority of real estate ads don't brand the agents for market recognition or actually sell the homes. But the herd keeps running them. This works to your advantage. The herd continues to pump out agent advertising featuring a laundry list of accolades and achievements that bore and bewilder the average prospect. Prospects just want to know, "Which agent cares, can relate to me, and will understand what I want?" The branded agent uses the 7 Branding Channels to tell a compelling story—a story that develops a connection with prospects acknowledging that they understand and are ready to help. The herd will mail out unbranded and unmemorable direct mail solicitations for business, usually once, and then give up, or try again next year. The herd is predictable, tired, and inconsistent. You will not be.

Branding is not a quick fix or a shortcut, but rather a steady, proactive, and thoughtful road to real estate success. To achieve lasting success in real estate you have to build your business on the solid foundation that the 7 Branding Channels provide. Are there other real estate marketing and advertising activities that you can employ to increase business? Sure, but these seven processes are the ingredients that will effectively establish your brand while still allowing you to continue the daily logistics of listing, selling, and servicing your clients. If, like most of the herd, you decide to incorporate only one or two channels, you will probably gain a modicum of success. But you will not even come close to the full blown success of the completely branded agent. The branded agent incorporates all seven channels into the business, so success is not limited by market conditions or chance. Once the groundwork for each channel has been laid, the branded agent is positioned for greater income, passion, and longevity. The herd never stops to do the groundwork, which is all the better for you.

Becoming your own personal real estate brand means executing different approaches to advertising and marketing. Through networking, you will start being personally involved with your target market and will begin to get valuable credit and recognition for doing so. You will become technologically proficient and active in your Internet exploitation of real estate information about your market. You will learn to implement a systematized process of branded direct mailers and target market specific mailing lists. Your campaign will apply cost saving venue-focused and niche-tailored ads.

Through developing the 7 Brand Channels visual identity, networking plan, advertising and direct mail campaigns, internet presence, public relations, and personal brochures, you can build the brand that changes your life. Confidence usually comes with success, but your confidence can come from knowing that these 7 Brand Channels are all you need to break away from the herd and start living large. You will get noticed, remembered, and chosen. The initial investment is both time and some money. The eventual payoff is much more time and much more money.

Chapter 6

Visual Brand Identity

Appearance and Style

Humans are visual people, and your personal brand must appeal to those senses. Most Americans watch TV much more than they read, and attention spans are getting shorter and shorter. The visual identity of a brand is what people think of when discussing the overall subject of "brand." The visual identity of your brand encompasses your appearance, style, and personality, in person and in the media. In person, what you wear, what you look like, how you present yourself, and how you sound are all part of your visual ID. In print or on screen your visual brand identity is found in the photos, colors, logos, tag lines, layouts, designs, copywriting, and standards that determine your message. By assimilating both the live you and your tools (ads, mailers, sites, brochures, etc.) consumers develop a perception of your brand. Your brand channels have to be consistent between the living version of You, Inc. and the advertised version of You, Inc.

We all judge and compartmentalize people and things all day. Branding takes advantage of that natural tendency. People size you up and brand you within seconds of seeing you or your marketing. The herd is not in control of the outcome, but the branded agent is. Personal branding is not about just dressing for success. You must create a look and style that resonates with your target market, a look that says "I get you. I understand the interests, values, and lifestyle of this, my target market." You have to differentiate from the herd *and* fit in with your target audience.

Having the right visual brand opens the door to being liked, believed, and trusted. Average agent qualities like negotiating skills or marketing insight cannot be determined by appearance, but that doesn't stop people from making assumptions about the lack or presence of such things. Your visual brand, the face and voice that represents you and what you stand for, is one of the most influential elements in your message.

Your consistent style serves to support the idea of You, Inc. with your target audience. How your clothes look, what you drive, where you live, how you walk into a room, and how you present yourself should all have a conscientious brand approach. Your appearance is the one thing that will always resonate with your target market. Your targeted consumers may not have had the benefit of a personal relationship with you yet. They may not have had the benefit of a real estate transaction demonstrating your service and standards. However, they will have had multiple exposures to your style through your branding channels or lack there of. Your target audience needs to understand, admire, appreciate, and relate to your appearance. Driving an SUV and wearing a fur while you target the environmental component of your area won't work. Consistency is one of the most influential keys to branding. Keep your style consistent with your brand if you hope to maintain an authentic edge over your competition.

Anyone can manipulate the power of visual attraction, because attraction doesn't depend solely on looks. In fact, according to a recent study by Markus Mobius of Harvard and Tanya Rosenblatt of Wesleyan, 15–20% of attraction is based on a perception of self confidence. Forty percent is attributed to a self-assured oral communication style, and the remaining 40% is affected by overall visual presence. According to that data, you can manipulate at least 60% of the standards by which you are judged. Confidence and oral communication skills are things that anyone can improve. Develop these skills; they'll go a long way towards creating credibility. These are some of the skills that separate you from the herd as it is the visual impact that determines how you are primarily perceived as an agent brand.

Your visual identity is your target market's easiest point of recognition. A visual ID creates the familiarity that can quickly shift people from prospects to clients. The strength of visual brand identity is undeniable. After all, what is Nike without the Swoosh or the "just do it" tagline? What is McDonald's without the golden arches? Commoditize yourself and use the same powerful concept to create positive brand association. Through personality, imagery, colors, logo, tagline, copy, and quality of production, you create the memorable brand packaging that emotionally connects you with your target market.

Photography

So far we still don't know which fine steward of business acumen started the realtor headshot trend, the concept sure did stick. Nothing says herd more than the predictable realtor mug shot. As an agent, your photograph is the single most identifiable element of your brand. Many people are self conscious about their appearance. But instead of doing the work to improve confidence, style, and presentation, the average agent will spend fifty bucks for the traditional real estate mug shot and figure the picture is good enough. They rationalize that making the investment to get a quality lifestyle image that best represents their brand is overkill, and continue to use the mundane headshot along with the rest of the agent population.

VISUAL BRAND IDENTITY

Your picture creates your personal brand perception. I cannot stress enough the importance of having a photograph that is unique, relevant to your target, friendly, and accessible. You can't accomplish that with the typical headshot. Using the same old stiff pose is the surest way to get lost in the crowd. Quality photography speaks directly to your standards in business. Some in the herd miss the mark and attempt to improve their images by using glamour shots taken twenty years ago. But the only message this sends is that the agent is too lazy to update the picture, doesn't have the resources to do so, or is embarrassed by their current look. None of these messages positively or authentically brands the agent's business.

Your lifestyle photo should be relaxed and natural. The purpose of using a personal photo in your business is not so that someone can pick you out of a line up. Leave the uptight pictures for the attorneys. You are selling personality and emotion. Your clothing and overall style don't determine how well you do your job, but they will have a significant impact on how well people *perceive* that you do your job. Above all, remain true to your authentic self. If you don't wear a suit in your daily business activities, don't wear a suit in your photograph. If prospects get to know your brand as a professional in a sophisticated suit, they won't know what to think if you come to an initial meeting in khakis and a polo shirt. People will come to know you by this photo, and if you fail to be yourself, you will appear phony and inconsistent. Don't confuse your clients before you even get to know them. You want to be sure to meet their expectations from the start.

Use a lifestyle picture, action shot, or an image that displays your approachability. Use a photo that captures your whole body (or at least from the waist up) as body language is important in expressing personality. Try to tie the characteristics of your target market into your photo through location or color. Use props sparingly. Leave cliché images like a golf club in hand or a pose with a sold sign to the herd. If golf is your thing, have a professional, high definition, full body photo with golf course residences in the background. Madras shorts and an orange Titlist lid can ruin a great outdoor location shot, so take the time to plan your wardrobe carefully.

Figuring out your shot is much easier once you know exactly how you want to be perceived by your target market. Try different positioning and posing ideas. Stay away from over-done "creative" editing like manipulating the colors or rotating images. Don't get paralyzed by picture selection, but be selective. Once your brand shot is chosen you need to use that image always to maintain brand consistency. If you switch between images, clients will take much longer to make the brand connection. The idea is to become a recognized brand expert as quickly as possible. Simplicity is crucial when reaching target market minds through multiple brand exposures.

VISUAL BRAND IDENTITY

Work until you get the perfect picture. Remember pick one brand shot and stick with it.

Hire a professional photographer for the job. High-resolution photography is critical. You will be using your brand imagery in newsletters, magazines, and brochures where high definition quality photography can be the difference between making a great first impression and falling flat. Reducing the size and resolution of the image for digital use on the Internet is easy, but you can't improve resolution and size if the picture is not originally captured with high resolution. Once your branded shot is selected, keep various sizes and formats available in a computer file so you can quickly retrieve the right image for all of your marketing.

Your personal brand imagery should be used everywhere for ultimate impact. Digitally, your photo will be used on email signatures, blogs, headers, E-newsletters, web pages, Internet articles, and other e-spots. Your image will be on printed materials like personal brochures, business cards, newsletters, direct mailers, ad campaigns, and promotional pieces. Don't publish another marketing piece until you give your personal photo the time needed to establish itself as the flagship of your brand's visual identity. Your personal photo is that important.

Your branded photo will be displayed throughout the seven branding channels to create consistent brand impressions of you as the professional, personable, hard working agent of choice. A powerful photograph can trigger all of these positive associations. You want your client base to see you as someone whom they would enjoy spending the day with searching for homes, and someone whom they would trust to sell their home. This may be your first or only chance to create a likable, relatable image. The only requirements of your personal photo are to mirror the appearance, style, and standard that defines your personal brand.

Colors

Color scheme is the next element necessary to create a complete branded visual identity. To the herd, colors are arbitrarily chosen and usually just a matter of personal preference. But can you imagine Target featuring a yellow bull's eye logo instead of a red one? Or what if UPS drivers delivered packages in red trucks? UPS is known as the Brown company. No other delivery startup can use that same shade. You want *your* brand colors to help you claim your place in the market as well. Color can be used to "paint" your turf, making breaking into your niche difficult or even impossible for the competition. In many cases, colors can be as defining as a logo or image. Choose a color or color combination that you're comfortable with, and that will complement your visual brand identity.

Just as you may have difficulty imagining your favorite sports team wearing the colors of their biggest rivals, using colors that are similar to your biggest competitors will create confusion within your target market, too. Also, try to avoid using colors that are too similar to that of your own real estate parent company. You are selling yourself, not the company. You do not want to have clients identify your brand and your company as one in the same. When you promote the company, you often lose control of prospects who call your company in response to *your* ads.

Stick to your real estate agency's guidelines for the placement and size of your company logo and information, but maintain your brand as the focus. If you are a one-person shop, then you and the company identity should be one brand. According to NAR statistics, the average span that an agent stays with one real estate company is only two years. The average is four years if the agent is a broker. Reinventing your brand every time you change companies will be costly and cripple the momentum you've established for your brand recognition. Worst of all, if your brand campaign consists of mostly institutional logos and colors, then valuable time and money will have been wasted, too.

I'm amazed that so many agents promote their companies more than they promote themselves. Look at the majority of agent websites; the first thing that you'll see is the company's logo, tagline, and colors. These sites are typically pre-fabricated "agent" templates paid for by the company. They are entirely made up of the company's fonts, colors, logos, and imagery. The sites are free but are also the same for every agent in the company.

The herd believes that these company tools are their ticket to online success. Trust me, take the control back, promote yourself, and let the company take a back seat for a while. Your goal is to become the agent of choice under a strong company umbrella. Consumers choose good agents over company popularity. Of course, when you are the realtor of choice, the company reaps the financial rewards.

Be aware of basic color psychology when creating your color palate.

- **Black** is the color of authority and power.
- **White** is light, neutral, and pure.
- **Red** is emotionally intense and actually increases heart rate and breathing. Red is associated with passion, fury, and love.
- **Blue** evokes a sense of calmness and serenity. Recognized as the color of the sky and sea, blue evokes a sense of tranquility and causes the body to produce calming chemicals.
- **Green** is also calming, refreshing, and relaxing. Green is associated with the environment, health, and money (many banks use green).
- **Yellow** enhances concentration, and represents optimism, but can be hard on the eyes depending on the shade and amount used.
- **Purple** has historically been associated with royalty and luxury.
- **Brown** is reliable, genuine, and earthy.

VISUAL BRAND IDENTITY

These color associations can help to relay positive emotions towards your personal brand.

Avoid the urge to use trendy colors or hues that may go out of style quickly. You are creating a brand that should be the foundation a lengthy career. Opt for the safe choice of time honored and traditional primary colors over custom colors. Of course, if you decide there is a Martha Stewart pale blue and sea green combination that effuses your brand perfectly into the minds of your target audience, you make that decision. To be sure, test the combination on your friends and colleagues. You might have created the perfect color combination for your brand. Usually, however, current popular color combinations and hues will have a shorter life span than traditional color combinations, which have a broader appeal. Just like the once popular fluorescent colors still scream the 80's, orange with pink will seem dated in a year or two, but classic combinations like navy and red or green and white will always be solid choices.

Also, stick with one or two prominent colors and one subtle background or accent color. More than three colors in your brand identity can be distracting and less appealing. Simplicity is almost always best. Test your scheme and theory on others and get their reactions.

Once chosen, incorporate your colors into your logo, ad and mailer layouts, internet site, business card, personal brochures, etc. Use the same shade, hue, and intensity of color throughout your brand from now on. The power of brand recognition, association, and perception is dependant on consistency. Your color scheme helps consumers quickly identify your brand during the daily onslaught of thousands of brand exposures.

Logo

Your logo provides another easily recognizable symbol of your brand identity. A powerful logo is so influential that even a quick glance can trigger positive thoughts about your brand. Chanel's interlocking C's, NBC's colorful peacock, Disney's black mouse ears, and Gerber's baby all create and re-stimulate emotional recognition every time they appear.

Many agents have never considered creating a personal logo. Logos are no longer reserved for large corporations. The advent of personal computing and the creative capabilities available have allowed even the smallest operation to utilize the marketing power of logos.

The logo is another weapon in your brand arsenal to create quick, positive recognition and a lasting impression in the minds of consumers. While your logo should be an attention grabber, make sure your design is created with the following standards in mind. A successful logo must:

VISUAL BRAND IDENTITY

1. Apply basic design fundamentals
2. Represent your brand message
3. Function across different media
4. Create a memorable impression

The first element of an effective logo is simplicity. Basic design fundamentals are crucial to success. Enlist the help of a professional graphic designer or artist to design your logo or improve one that you've created. Designers have a better understanding of basic design elements like space, form, consistency, color and clarity. Their experience will give your logo a professional and effective appearance. If you don't have the budget for a designer, take a close look at other successful logos. Take note of the elements that stand out to you and try to determine what makes those logos work so well. Determine which logos work for you and why. A clean, simple logo is more eye-catching than a busy one. If your logo is too busy, your audience will have a hard time recognizing the image. The professional look of your logo is directly associated with the professionalism of your service.

Your logo must reflect your brand message. If your brand is bold and expressive, then your fonts and colors should be as well. If you specialize in Victorian homes, you wouldn't want a heavy block font and design. An ornate font and an elegant image would best convey your brand. In order to design a logo that best represents your brand, take a close look at the characteristics that make your target market special. If your target market is a geographic niche then consider using a landmark or scenic design that consumers would recognize and appreciate.

Be careful about incorporating your own name into your logo. Only use word-plays if your name fits well with the theme. Unless Chuck Chapel sells renovated churches as residences, then his use of a church steeple as his logo is clever and memorable, but probably not consistent with his target market. Chuck would be better off designing a logo around his target niche. Cute name associations are complicated, but not out of the question. You can use a name-association logo as long as the design meets the four standards above. Simple designs based on the agent's name or initials can resonate well with the target audience. Both IBM and Coca-Cola logos are simple variations of their respective company names.

When developing your logo, don't be afraid to think outside the box. What is your brand message? Who are you targeting? What is important to your clients? The image or symbol doesn't have to be unique, but the significance and association with your overall brand should be clear.

Also, remember to make sure your logo is functional. The design will need to be used in a variety of media- print, online, and everywhere in between. The size could vary from an inch high to poster size. To be consistently effective your logo should be as clear and distinguishable on a promotional pen as on your company letterhead. The parameters and look of design should not change when the logo is resized or reformatted. Just as with your photo, keep a file with several usable versions of your logo in different sizes and formats (TIFF, PDF, JPG etc.) for quick email attachments and ad designs.

If some of these technical terms scare you, they shouldn't. Learning the processes is actually very simple. To find out about formatting and resizing images, take a class, read a guide, or even get short tutorials online. You are a marketer first. Selling homes is the result of your marketing and branding efforts. If you can't handle learning the skills necessary to efficiently utilize the seven brand channels, then you will not become a truly branded agent. You will be herded into the mass agent population and remain unnoticed. The technical aspects of managing logo and photo files are not nearly as intimidating as you think. With advanced Windows and Mac technology, the extent of your skill should include no more than being able to drag and drop files into the right place. Don't be paralyzed in the middle of the herd because you think photos and file management is over your head. Dive in, you'll be amazed at how easily you learn, which will energize your commitment to your brand.

Your logo is another trigger for positive recognition and increased familiarity with your clients. So your logo has to be memorable. If you have followed the steps above by adhering to appropriate style and form, color scheme, and message, then making your logo memorable should be simple. Be original; your logo should not resemble anyone else's. Unlike your photo, which speaks of you, your logo speaks *to your market*. If the design doesn't resonate with your market, they will not remember your brand. Test your logo with friends and family to see if they think the image will reverberate with a certain target market.

Tagline

Unlike a photo and a logo, which reflect imagery, a tagline allows you to use words to communicate. Mention, "Where's the beef?" "Don't leave home with out it." or "Melts in your mouth, not in your hand," and you immediately register Wendy's, American Express, and M&M's. By incorporating a tagline, you further define and emphasize your brand message. Your logo and tagline may complement each other, which allow them to be used together or individually throughout your campaign. Sometimes tag lines are incorporated directly into the logo design. But there are also situations when just your branded tagline at the end of a blog or ad is more appropriate or compelling than a logo. A tagline should be memorable, short, and direct. Use these questions to help craft your slogan:

> *Who is your target market?*
> *What benefits do you provide them?*
> *What is unique about your brand?*

VISUAL BRAND IDENTITY

How do you differ from the competition?
What feelings do you hope to evoke in your consumers?
What is the purpose of your brand/business?

Hopefully you have already answered these questions while reading the section, "Discovering Your Brand." Write several short phrases that sum up your answers and encompass your brand message. "A history of results in Bergen County" is a geographic target specific tagline. "Foundations built on trust" would be target specific for new home sales. "Artistically uniting people and places" would be target specific to an agent targeting an artistic or cultural market of buyers and sellers in an area. Rhyming and alliteration can attract more attention and be memorable, but only if the lines contribute to the brand message. A couple of familiar examples are: "Takes a licking and keeps on ticking" or "Don't get mad, get Glad."

Your slogan should reflect your brand's personality, relay a key benefit, and remain simple and catchy all at the same time. This may seem tricky, but you'll be surprised what you can come up with once you begin the brainstorming process. Don't just settle for good. Work and test your brand to discover your best.

Copywriting

Emotionally persuasive copy has further positioned brands like Rolex and Hallmark ahead of their competitors. Great copy can take your brand beyond what taglines, photos, and logos can achieve. Through telling aspects of the brand story, copywriting establishes even deeper associations and positive perceptions with target markets. Great copywriting engages consumer sentiment. A single paragraph version of the brand story, along with a longer, multiple paragraph version of the same brand message should always be on hand.

Your relatable copy is essentially the written version of your brand elevator speech. How do you best tell the significant story of your brand- The story of You, Inc.? If someone takes the time to read your copy, you must reward their effort with an emotional incentive. People won't bother to develop a relationship with you when you brag about your accomplishments, but they will connect with your thoughtful story. Luxury brands Rolex and DeBeers understand the power of storytelling to influence their target market. For Rolex, prestige, desire, and power are essential elements of the story used to create emotional significance in the minds of consumers. DeBeers takes a different approach, using copy that appeals to the emotions associated with receiving a DeBeers masterpiece from a loved one. Nike has also recently jumped on the story bandwagon to promote their women's line. The new ads go beyond the male inspired "Just do it." slogan. Nike's new copy tells stories of empowered athletic women and targets a female market that emotionally connects with the product. This approach has driven the sales of Nike women apparel through the roof.

Your brand copy should never be confused with your résumé. Résumés are mundane, and your brand story must be interesting to your niche market. Your brand copy is your chance to let your target market know who you are and what you're all about. Be careful to avoid the common mistake of turning the story into a list of accomplishments and milestones.

Tell stories about your journey and lessons that have made you better. Weave in information about organizations that you're involved with, schools that you've attended, and places that you've lived. Describe family history and events that marked your path. Be professional and positive. Keep the story interesting and authentic, and always with brand message in mind. Highlight commonalities like your associations with and interests in your target market. The more opportunities you create to relate with your audience, the better. Your brand copy should be written as if someone else was telling the story about you and your business. Third person allows you to touch on your successes in a way that is less aggressive and more credible.

Once crafted, you will use your copy to enhance your unique brand identity everywhere possible. Your copy will be the guts of your personal brochure. Copy will be the "about" link on your website. The story will be your introduction at speaking engagements and meetings. Your brand copy is proof that if you do the hard work well, your upfront investment will take off and allow you to simply "Be your Brand."

Layout and design

Layout and design consists of the when, where, and how you will incorporate your visual brand identity into the various outgoing pieces from each branding channel. The goal is to have all materials working both individually and in conjunction with each other. Brand impressions have more impact when the integrity of brand consistency is carried through a number of different mediums. Cohesive brand exposures in print, through the mail, online, in person, and by word of mouth eliminate buyer resistance and elevate brand positioning exponentially over just one channel of advertising and marketing. Leave the overall concept of your layouts, from web site to mailers, to a professional designer who understands the aspects that make up your visual brand identity, and the importance of how they are arranged and delivered throughout the seven channels. You should only have to pay a professional for this help once though, because once it's perfect you'll stick with it.

In general, few, if any, people scout advertisements, wait for mailers, or even statistically look online to choose an agent to help them with real estate. Your branding work is not done in hopes of catching someone right as he or she is making a decision to buy or sell. Your branding work is done to create a perception you are the go-to agent, so that when the time comes to make a decision, the person thinks of you first.

Generally, the simpler and cleaner designs are the most effective. Crowded and complex ads can be offensive to the eye. Most of the time, less is more. The herd loves cramming a lot of stuff into an ad, and they will try a new layout every week until they start getting calls. Changing layouts confuses consumers and does not help to register your brand. Understand and remember that a brand doesn't take hold until after multiple, consistent impressions.

Of course, I personally recommend the resources at the Branded Cow Real Estate Branding Company. The "brand in a box" complete agent design solution is an aggressive head start to becoming a branded agent. The system offers a valuable solution to get you up and running with your own brand imagery including a personalized logo, tagline, and ad templates that are all ready to print. As with any aspect of your brand, once you have a layout for your various ads and copy written material, stick with them. Constant repetition to your target market builds familiarity and acceptance.

Standards

Quality is a standard by which you must gauge your brand identity. From appearance and style to layout, design, copy and production, quality must be an adjective that people associate with your brand. People yearn for quality in the products and services they purchase these days. Never forego quality for speed of delivery when developing your brand.

Take the time to build a quality foundation for all the channels and particularly the aspects of your visual brand identity. If you invest time and money to create the perfect photo, logo, tag line, and design, don't waste what you've done by unveiling the brand to your target market in poor quality. Your prospects will naturally assume that if you've cut corners on your marketing materials, you will cut corners in your service to them. For example, weight, type of stock, sheen, and size are just a few of the decisions you have to make on paper selection for a particular branding solution. Again, the good news is that if you take the time to choose right the first time you won't have to start over.

Quality in branding doesn't necessarily have to cost more if you provide the elbow grease up front. You can cut costs by knowing your brand design. Having direct mail and ad templates allows you to order larger quantities of printing material at lower prices. Branded templates let you simply drag and drop information, which saves ongoing production costs. And quality branded ad templates can make the same impact with smaller ads and fewer runs when supported by the other ongoing brand channel campaigns. Skimping anywhere on quality will be detrimental to your brand. Pay for the quality, and the investment will be returned. The care you have for the quality of your visual branding identity translates to the care and quality standards you put into the services your offer.

Chapter 7

Networking

With most opportunities today, what you know is not as important as who you know. Many sales people boast about their networking skills, but very few actually understand what the word means. The herd habitually overlooks the powerful impact of networking. Traditionally, 40% of an agent's business comes from referrals, but even many branded agents don't place enough value and time on networking. Networking is an authentic way to demonstrate that you are an approachable businessperson who has a passion for your specialty. Those that have mastered networking know that their success relies on helping others in any way they can, as they will receive similar reciprocation.

Networking, which is when referrals are exchanged, brand identity, and credibility are built on a personal level. Successful networking is a two way street where you become the conduit to help others make beneficial connections. Living your brand through involvement in associations, activities, leadership roles, and events will reward you infinitely. Networking builds relationships, increases the number of referrals, and reinforces you as the obvious expert in your market. Networking is a personal way to brand within your niche while enjoying the activities that interest you and those individuals in your target market. Building relationships based on things that you all have in common allows the relationships to develop naturally. As people get to know you as a trusted friend and resource, they will feel comfortable referring you, their preferred expert, to friends and family.

One of the most effective ways to show that you care about your prospects is to Network within your specialization well and often. You may feel like this is self-serving at first, but networking is actually just the opposite. Opportunities abound to volunteer, support, lead, join, and socialize within your market. These are value added ways to infiltrate your target market and to add credibility and trust to your personal brand. The key is to stick to the organizations and events that you truly enjoy and are passionate about. This should not be hard if you have aligned your interests and values to a corresponding target market discussed in part one, "Discovering Your Brand." If there isn't an organization in place already, create one. Starting an organization that directly relates to your target market in a relevant way is one of the best ways to get recognized as the expert in your specialty market. Creating an organization is also a great public relations move, which we'll discuss in the sixth branding channel.

Networking activities help participants grow their business through mutual referrals and informative discussions on topics such as positioning, products, and marketing. Business networking clubs are one of the most popular and recognizable groups to join or start. These organizations are full of influential people who understand the power of relationships and referrals. Networking is not about mindless small talk, but rather about discussing strategies and sharing information. You will have a chance to provide valuable real estate services, advice, and guidance to professionals in other businesses. And you will get recognized for doing so. Through time spent together, business club and association members develop strong and trusting relationships, and a strong foundation for referral exchange. The potential reach here is infinite, as you not only refer to the immediate contacts, but you can also count on their referrals within each of their own personal and business circles.

If they are willing, get your family members involved as well. Family values are at the core of many real estate target markets. Showing that you enjoy spending time with your family resonates with others that share your values. The more people your spouse and children meet, the stronger your brand identity will become. Don't get me wrong, you're not putting your family to work for you. But the fact is that the more people see you as a father or mother, husband or wife, the more approachable and relatable you will appear.

Your family represents the side of your brand that is honest, approachable, and real. When people see you in a family environment, they are less intimidated by the fact that you are a salesperson. This is a valuable impression that helps discourage sales resistance. The next time someone asks for the name of a good realtor, it may well be the combination of your respected business and trustworthy family ties that make you the agent first in mind. A note here, your networking involvement and subsequent actions are only disingenuous if you are inauthentic in your motivation or are only involved for the money. These networking opportunities are win-win situations made possible by the alignment of values and interests in your area of specialty. People can spot a fraud a mile away. If you fake enthusiasm, you may as well forget a positive reaction.

Good networking employs a type of "pay it forward mentality." Remember the last time someone referred business to you, bought you lunch, or gave you an unsolicited compliment in front of a colleague, boss, or potential consumer? How did that make you feel? Most people not only feel grateful in these situations, but they genuinely want to reciprocate the good will. Your gesture won't be forgotten, and the people you help out will want to help you in return. The more business you refer to someone you trust, the more business the recipient of your generosity will want to refer to you. The more people you can move into this type of relationship, the more referrals you will garner. Call the phenomenon Karma or whatever you like, but doing things for others offers more benefits than just warm fuzzies. Goodwill and generosity bring you more business, better relationships, an elevated level of respect, and a more powerful brand.

In general, never take a referral relationship for granted. Nurture the relationship as you would that of your very best client. Be proactive in sending thank you cards and gifts, take friends and colleagues to dinner, visit when appropriate, help to establish business connections, and by all means send them referrals too. Make these important contacts part of your sphere of influence, a group that you interact and communicate with regularly. This work and time should be a major focus of your master branding plan.

Beyond mutual referral farming, networking gives you ample opportunity to further elevate the perception of your professional brand by what you accomplish within your networking groups. Usually the creation of an event that raises money for a local cause is a good place to start. Besides the rewards of helping others, you meet and interact with more people, which allows you to grow your brand's visibility. Charity events allow you to showcase and bolster your authentic brand, while doing something that enriches your own existence. Events that benefit others enforce strong brand positioning. Your involvement and leadership in important projects suggest that you must be an approachable, relatable, and caring person.

Networking online provides opportunities as well, but the job is tougher since connecting with people is really an interpersonal skill that requires live meetings. But there are sites like, LinkedIn and Plaxo, along with dozens of others that offer business networking for executives and business folks. These sites are akin to popular social networking sites like Facebook or MySpace, which may be beneficial too depending upon the target market. Other than being a feature rich online address book, the premise of these sites is to grow your network through principles similar to the six degrees of separation. You add to your network through online interaction, needs, introductions, research, and invitations. The advantage is that this provides another way to maintain contacts and relationships with people who obviously value that avenue of interaction.

There are plenty of great books available on the art of networking and countless approaches to networking well. Your challenge is to just get involved. Activities and interests like tennis, gardening, cooking, and worship are all great ways to meet new people and foster relationships around your community. Book clubs, knitting, or dining out groups also work well and are a lot of fun. More structured organizations like PTA, neighborhood associations, school boards, and political committees are also brand worthy and rewarding. Check your local paper or town hall, and ask around. You should be excited by the opportunities to create fulfilling and beneficial relationships.

One big pitfall of networking is the tendency to alienate others by having strong and imposing opinions about organizational activities or purpose. Having comportment is the characteristic necessary to successfully navigate the minefields of organized groups. Just as listening is a primary sales skill, paying attention is your best networking trait, too.

Networking is the greatest opportunity for you to showcase your appearance and style in person. Make a positive impression every time. You are always branding. People may or may not care that you are a technically skilled agent, but they will most certainly care that you treat their referrals well. Because they personally recommended you, their reputations are on the line. They need to trust that you will keep your promises and meet their expectations. People love to be heard, so show some love and keep any potentially divisive thoughts in your noggin. Remember, 40% of real estate business comes from referrals. Networking should get at least that much of your effort.

Chapter 8

Advertising

Paying for placement to elevate and expose your brand to your target audience is a costly but necessary channel in brand building. Consistent exposure to your brand and message creates familiarity. I've said this before: people do business with *familiar* salespeople and companies. The advantage of having a brand and specialty is that whatever the medium, you can focus the venue and tailor the message.

Advertising is paralyzing to most of the agent population. There are so many opportunities to advertise, that instead of developing a plan, agents tend to haphazardly advertise with no real objective in place. This approach is incredibly dangerous and can deplete a budget quickly with little return on the investment. Some agents opt for the cheapest opportunities with no defined target market, which wastes money by reaching the wrong people.

Be cautious of real estate-specific magazines that simply showcase area properties. At first glance, they may seem like the perfect outlet to reach potential buyers, but they really do very little to support your brand. They reach a broader spectrum of the population than is really necessary, and the readers are typically more interested in the homes than in the agents. These magazines typically do not get regular readership, so the consistent impressions you are hoping to gain do not happen. Overall, your investment is better spent elsewhere. The key is to discover the publications that your niche regularly reads and enjoys. The more specialized the medium, the more you'll be associated with your niche market. Advertise where your clients feel at home.

Another mistake agents make is to spend the entire advertising budget on the local newspaper's real estate section. The return is rarely worth the costly investment. These ads rarely make the phone ring with interested buyers. Newspaper advertising has become one of the most ineffective opportunities available. Many in the herd even know the math: the Sunday paper has proven to produce only a 2% return at best. Most of the herd can't stop the cycle. They continue wasting money advertising their listings in an attempt to satisfy their client's expectations. Homeowners like seeing their homes pictured in the paper. But your responsibility as an agent is to educate home sellers. Teach them where the best advertising opportunities are and why. Show them that you have the same goal in mind – to sell their home quickly and profitably. Branded agents explain to their clients that homebuyers no longer wait to get property listings from the newspaper. Information moves much more quickly now, and today's homebuyer would rather see multiple high resolution photos, virtual tours, tax records, and full property descriptions than make decisions based on a tiny newspaper photo. As such, 80% of buyers now search online.

The herd is afraid to educate their sellers to the benefit of their business. Branded agents take the substantial amount of money they *don't* waste on newspaper ads to properly fund strategic internet partnerships and targeted advertising for their brand instead. Branded agents brand first and sell second. Advertising is expensive and seldom sells homes, but it is one of the most powerful tools to strengthen your brand identity.

There is some value in showing listings in ads these days. Doing so demonstrates that you are a busy bee and have some experience listing homes- See! Look, here they are! If this is your reasoning for spending money to advertise pictures of homes, then make sure your brand garners most, if not all, of the ad's attention.

Even when you understand the use for print advertising, you still have a lot of decisions to make, considering the exhaustive amount of opportunities. Knowing your target markets allows you to tailor your message, which saves you money by substantially increasing the return on your investment. Focus your advertising dollars on placement that specifically reaches your target market. For example, don't pay to advertise all over the state if your niche is a small part of one county. Don't pay for expensive, glossy magazine placement if your target market doesn't read that publication. Bigger is not better when branded advertising is concerned.

Branded agents are found in targeted trade magazines, weekly community papers, and target-specific newsletters. For example, if your niche focuses on a lifestyle like golf course communities, advertise in relative venues. Consider sponsoring a tournament or advertising in a local golf magazine, country club newsletter, or community magazine. If you specialize in a geographic community, advertise in the neighborhood newspaper and school programs. If you specialize in a demographic like teachers, the local teaching or trade product catalog is a perfect venue for advertising, or you can sponsor education related programs. Specialized publications are less expensive, have less competition, and a much longer shelf life. They are a strong alternative to local newspapers and have much higher returns.

Some other advertising options include television and radio commercials, billboards, or event sponsorships. Television commercials, while prestigious and far reaching are typically one of the most costly advertising forums. TV can be a great way to showcase your personality or provide client testimonials but can often be tougher to pinpoint a specific group of consumers. For most agents, the cost in this case will outweigh the results.

If you want to showcase your personality or give client testimonials, put video or audio ads on your website, instead of investing in the big budget media. A few branded agents have gotten big enough in large markets that the return on radio and TV exposure supports the cost, but not without some risk. Similarly, advertising on billboards and benches works well for a few agents but is not suited for most. There are plenty of ideas to expose your brand, but the trick is to have a comprehensive plan to be able to discover the maximum potential for each channel while staying solvent and focusing on your business.

Be selective with event or team sponsorships. Make sure they fit your niche, and keep them network focused. People are always looking for sponsors, and learning to say no to the opportunities that don't align with your brand could be the difference between making a profit and not. If the deal isn't right for you, always refer the opportunity to someone who can benefit from the sponsorship. This is an excellent way to network and help out those seeking sponsors rather than just saying no.

Once you focus your advertising dollars to best reach your niche, you can work on tailoring your advertisement to resonate with your target market. You've got the right placement, now you have to design memorable advertisements. Don't worry if your ad doesn't click with anyone outside of your target market. If the ad speaks only to your target market, you can be sure the ad is a good one. Your ad should be templated, incorporating your photo, logo, tagline, design, and a little contact and company information. Decide on a format that will best tell your story in a glance. You also want a design that will retain its integrity when modified to fit different layouts.

Advertising in real estate is a channel that must be budgeted, as there are endless solicitations and opportunities to advertise. If more ads meant more referrals, then running more ads would make sense, but that is not the case. John Wanamaker said, "Half of the money I spend on advertising is wasted. The trouble is, I just don't know which half." In most cases advertising is trackable, so take charge of your campaign by monitoring your ads. Tracking the return on branded ads will help determine if you are profiting from your advertising choices at the end of the year.

At least 15% of your income should be invested in personal branding. Advertising will use up the majority of your ongoing brand investment. Staying on budget is vital, so keep in mind that you don't have to be in every run or issue of the advertising publication that you pick. For example, when there is a weekly neighborhood newspaper that has good readership by your target market, but you can't afford to advertise weekly, try advertising bi-weekly.

ADVERTISING

Most people won't realize that you aren't featured in the paper every week. Your ad template is consistent, so instead of recognizing when you aren't there, consumers will only notice when you are. You can stay on budget while remaining effective and consistent in your advertising approach.

Changing your advertising campaign halfway through or being inconsistent in venues will only confuse your targeted market. Many agents get frustrated in their campaigns after a few months of receiving only minimal response. But the worst thing you can do is fail to see your campaign through. You have to make the commitment up front to give your campaign at least a year before pulling the plug or making any drastic changes. Advertising is a long process of branding, rarely a short term solution for sales.

If you've tried an ad for an appropriate amount of time and decide you need to make changes, be smart. Many agents change ad designs when they don't think they are right or working properly. Changing branded ads only restarts the process of brand recognition. Every time you make distinct changes, your audience has to adjust. Subtle changes to design and layout won't kill brand positioning, but they won't help very much either. The best advice is to get the ad as close to perfect as possible from the beginning and go with it. Branded agents should pick their design, set a brand template, and let the ads do the work.

Advertising keeps your brand in the minds of your target market and reinforces the branding work done by the six other channels. Advertising reminds everyone that the expert is available and ready to help. Advertise your *brand* for long term recognition, not your listings for short term failure.

Chapter 9

Direct Mail Marketing

Direct mail is the most focused marketing approach. Designed to reach specific target markets, direct mail includes postcards, newsletters, and promotional pieces that are mailed to a chosen group of recipients. Direct mail marketing is a valuable tool for creating strong impressions and establishing yourself as a credible market leader.

Direct mail is a crucial aspect in creating brand impressions within your target market. Mailing your ads allows you to choose an exact group of clients to target, while remaining cost efficient. The beauty behind direct mail marketing is that you are always in control. You can decide who to target, what to send, how often, and when you'd like your target market to receive the message. There aren't deadlines to worry about, materials won't be wasted on an unintended audience, and you can customize your marketing to fit your brand message.

BRANDING

While large mailings can be expensive to produce and deliver, targeting and using a template reduces costs significantly. As always, consistency in design and delivery is vital. Postcards work best, because they don't need to be opened to make a brand impact. When you send branded postcards, your consumers can get all the information they need from a quick glance, even as the card is on the way to the trash. Typically with branded direct mail, you only have a few seconds for your target market to absorb your brand message. Use this time to remind them that you are still the expert, and you are out there working hard.

First, your plan should include a database of your target market. Your direct mail list should consist of your entire target market and sphere of influence, which includes your networking contacts, prospects, clients, vendors, ancillary support, friends, family, and colleagues that you interact with regularly. Your database is the lifeblood of your business. You must have a complete sphere list that is updated regularly.

Thanks to new technology, building and running your system is much easier and less time consuming than older programs. Express Copy, Quantum Mail, and other companies will let you keep your template and your mail list online. Branded agents don't need to be graphic designers, labelers, or mail carriers. With the right programs, you can cut and paste or drag and drop your info into your brand template and let it rip.

Title companies and property tax search sites offer easy ways to create targeted geographic lists. Demographic lists take more work to compile than a basic geographical niche would, but the work will separate your brand from the herd. But even with these simple logistics, agents seem to get stuck and fail to be consistent. A successful direct mail branding channel is contingent on the strength of the mailing list. You may need a few weeks to compile the perfect list, but once the list is created, the hardest work will be done.

Similar to print ads, direct mailers don't sell homes. They work to make you the most recognizable agent. Your success is dependent on the regularity and consistency of your mailings. Contacting a potential client once or even sporadically will make success very unlikely. Twelve mailings a year should be your minimum. You are going to set yourself apart from the pack by consistently adding to your brand equity. This can't be said enough. Your consistent approach is what will determine your success. So many agents try these programs for a couple months and give up. The best agents know that success is so simple when you learn to see your strategy through to the end.

Your mailing campaign should consist of just listed, just sold, and niche specific information cards as well as customized newsletters. These particular pieces work together to create impressions that consistently brand you as the leader, the expert, and the go-to agent for that market. Your direct mail design should look exactly like your advertising and Internet presence. Your just listed and just sold cards, newsletters, and market specific informational postcards should all have exactly the same branded look that is supported by your other ongoing brand channel campaigns. This way you ensure that each piece registers with your market as a part of your brand collection, no matter how fast the mailing gets tossed.

Just Listed and Just Sold Cards

Just Listed and Just Sold cards are one of the best ways to position your brand as a market leader. They are also an easy place to start a branded direct mail campaign, especially if you have a few listings and sales to promote. Beginning with your branded direct mail template, simply plug in the title, address, and photos. Then print and mail. Because your template is already pre-set specifically for postcards, the process takes little time, but it still reinforces the targeted branded impression that you are out there dependably getting the job done.

Post cards are effective even if they feature a property you've sold outside of your market. Anything that reminds people that you are busy and successful at work is good branding. Postcards maximize that five-second opportunity to get your prospects' attention as they flip through the day's mail. Consumers equate high activity rates with success, and everybody wants to use the services of a successful agent.

More agents should take advantage of this simple marketing tactic. Postcards provide an opportunity for you to show your niche market that you are a top performer without actually having you sing your own praises. Postcards allow your target market to make their own conclusions about your success. These direct mail brand impressions will have greater impact, because people feel more connected to their own personal decisions.

Some agents continue to make one crucial mistake. They don't brand their pieces. Yes, they may put their photo and company logo on the card, and they may even add a tagline, but that doesn't do much if the marketing isn't consistently adding to their brand equity or number of impressions.

Just Listed and Just Sold cards are also good because they create the impression that you are selling even more than you are. Obviously, a lot of the postcards you send out will get thrown away quickly. If you are sending out branded pieces, however, your materials will still register with most people even on the way to the trash. While unbranded realtors may be mailing the same number of pieces as you, their marketing won't continuously register with the niche. Because your audience won't always take the time to read your postcards, they will just assume that you've sold another property when they get new mailings from you. The next time a friend asks them if they know a good realtor, they will remember you from your branded mailings.

Newsletters

One of the biggest complaints about realtors today is that they don't communicate well or often enough. A newsletter is the ideal instrument to stay in constant contact with past, current, and future clients. You can feed your audience information on market trends, new technology, industry data, and specifics on your unique services. Using a newsletter is an impressive way to solidify your status as the realtor of choice without being intrusive or pushy.

People don't want to be sold on a product, they want easy access to clear information that helps them make their own decisions. Consumers are busy and don't appreciate being bothered or interrupted. Decades of being bombarded with pushy sales scripts and closing techniques have left people skeptical and tired. By offering relevant and timely information, you add value to your brand relationship. Useful facts can improve the lives of your prospective clients and position you as a valuable resource to your market. Give your audience interesting data that they can review at their leisure, and you will quickly be considered a local expert.

As with all of your advertising, you should work with templates to streamline production. There are companies and web sites that will let you build and upload your newsletter template and prepare the final product online. Then they will print and mail the newsletter to the people on a list you've created from their direct mailing database. Stay away from completely pre-packaged newsletters. Canned, third party production newsletters are not personalized or tailored to fit your brand. A well-formatted, professional brand template with original and thoughtful content is the way to go.

Your newsletter is as much a part of your brand as your logo or marketing. Again the format should maintain the same look, style, and feel that you've built throughout your branding channels. In addition, your newsletter should be designed to receive positive consumer response. The following steps will help you design a consistent newsletter that will brand you as a reliable expert and educate your readers.

1. Purpose. Ask yourself, "What is important to my audience?" and "What is my goal for creating this newsletter?" These questions will enable you to maintain focus throughout your newsletter while meeting your objectives.

2. Name. You must create a name for your newsletter that is catchy and relevant. Consider using a name, message, or idea that relates to your niche. For example, use a title like: "Joe Smith's Community News" or "The Providence Pulse."

3. Format. Clean and simple designs work best. Have a designer create the template, or create your own if you are proficient in design. Typically, you should include a title header, a table of contents, useful tips section, articles, news, statistics, trends, services, events, contact information, etc. Templates can be easily created and modified in programs like Microsoft Word or Publisher. Having your newsletter professionally printed on heavy stock paper with a high gloss finish reflects your brand best. Stick with the same sections and themes for all of your newsletters. Consistency in design also reiterates the impression that there is consistency in your service and brand.

4. Content. This is the real meat of your newsletter and should be as resourceful to your readers as possible. Go back to your initial niche research and focus on the topics that most appeal to your targeted audience. Keep in mind that your newsletter should interest, educate, and entertain. The worst thing you can do is write a lot of fluff that will leave your readers disappointed and annoyed that they took the time to read it.

Remember that you're working on building loyalty, so be careful not to focus too much on selling your business. An effective newsletter leads with information and only subtly promotes you and your services. Offer tips and bulleted lists on relevant topics, and keep the content somewhat simple and light. Write about networking contacts and events and include pictures of community members in action. Your networking contacts will appreciate the publicity and possible referral opportunities you have given them. Be positive and add humor if possible, but keep your tone very professional. Include articles on things like lawn care, decorating, upkeep, the environment, and energy efficiency. Borrowing content from other publications is appropriate when the topic is pertinent to your intended audience, but make sure you credit the source and get permission when required.

Get people involved. Adding quizzes, trivia, or other contests are simple ways to keep them engaged. Don't forget to use some space to promote your listings to remind your reader that you are a busy professional. You want to provide enough interesting and useful information to ensure that your readers won't get bored and will look forward to your next publication. Always refer to your website for additional information and archived newsletters. Also, your newsletter is a great place to reprint any brand press or publicity you've received.

5. Frequency. Offer your newsletter on a regular basis—weekly, monthly, or quarterly. Whatever schedule you choose, stick to that plan. A bi-weekly newsletter is a promise of a newsletter every other week. If you slack off and don't deliver on time, the perception will be that your brand doesn't follow through on its promises. Monthly if possible is solid newsletter frequency and good brand exposure.

6. Personalize. There are many great programs available that will provide you with newsletter articles, but original relevant content is best. A few canned articles of homeowner interest will be okay, but too much non-specific general info and your newsletter will lose appeal. Focus on personally writing the feature articles and commentary, and keep the pre-written pieces for the secondary space in your newsletter.

7. Proof. Too many people invest a lot of time and energy into creating the perfect newsletter and then don't proofread the final copy before mailing. Obviously, spelling and grammatical mistakes reflect badly on the brand. Your newsletter is a reflection of your brand. If the content is full of mistakes, you will be viewed as unprofessional or incompetent. Whether published in print, online, or both, your newsletter should be consistent in design and distribution. For regular exposure, space your newsletter mailings apart from your postcard mailings. Like other brand channels, a good newsletter is designed to raise the perception of your brand and help you become the Realtor of choice.

Niche Specific Postcards

Other good direct mail postcard ideas are market updates, announcements, and other concise mailings that provide useful information specific to your niche. Local schedules such as high school football, golf tournaments, or community events are good postcard mailers to tie your brand effectively to the market. People tend to hold onto these types of mailer longer as well. Your authentic interest in your target market should give you useful information for these mailings.

Promote anything that demonstrates that you are well informed about your target market. The information, tips, or event calendars need to be small enough to fit on your branded postcard template, which is something to keep in mind when creating the template. Keep the design and content simple and useful. Send items that your market can use and easily post on the bulletin board. Becoming a resource in your area of expertise can lead you to many fantastic opportunities down the road, so don't keep the information to yourself, share.

Direct mail continues to be a consistent method for branding today. The cost effective approach is perfect for creating impressions in the minds of your specialized market, is easy to implement, and allows you to be in control. By combining Just Listed and Just Sold postcards with the consistent monthly newsletter, and by filling in any gaps with niche specific postcards, you will have a direct mail campaign that will consistently brand you as the local expert. Even if most postcards only get you a few seconds of focused attention and brand recognition, that is a few seconds more than the average agent will get all year.

Chapter 10

Internet Marketing

Internet technology and virtual communication is continually instrumental in positioning you as the brand of choice in your target market. Your Internet presence gives you the ability to become an effective resource for many of your consumers. Prospective buyers visit your site to find out about schools, lifestyle, statistics, data, and, most importantly, to see homes. Sellers use the Internet to see how you market your listings on the web and to view competing listings. Clients visit to find pertinent information regarding contracts, closings, utilities, and relocation.

Websites

For real estate agents in today's market, a website is a *must*. The Internet reaches the broadest spectrum of potential clients, is cost effective, customizable, and can still be focused. According to NAR, 80% of homebuyers begin their home search online. Obviously, the Web provides a great opportunity to build your brand identity with consumers. Creating a user friendly website that is both informative and effective as a sales and marketing tool is key for you to further enhance your brand positioning and create leads.

Web pages offer you another channel to further define your brand identity. They are platforms from which you can present the other six channels of your brand. Your branded photos, colors, tag lines, and design should provide the actual layout and feel of the site. Your copy should comprise the content of your "about" page. Include links to your social networking contacts and your off line networking activities.

Most clients no longer need very much agent assistance. With access to so many tools, many are doing their own upfront research, so branded agents have to seize the positions still available on the new playing field. Your site must deliver prospects with effective search tools and eye-catching search results. That means you should not require registration to use your site or to search. The old school of thought was that you could get people to sign-in or register to tour your site, which allowed you to collect contact information for possible leads. But a registration form is the number one turnoff to prospects who want quick and easy information.

At the early search stage most people just want information and aren't ready to open themselves up to salespeople yet. And they don't have to. There are plenty of sites that offer a variety of search options and benefits with no sign-in or registration. These are the sites that get the most traffic. Your best bet is to provide the best search solution and hope for loyalty from those who have benefited from your site.

You can virtually offer links to most anything on the web, and you should use these links to offer relevant information and resources to your clients and prospects. Link to your blog and articles you've written. Offer a link to a printable copy of your personal brochure, direct mail newsletter, market update posts, and to current brand press and publicity. Other links should include an informational page for current clients to refer to for utility information, license and registration, and important dates, addresses, and numbers. Your web address should appear everywhere that your phone number appears. Offer a page explaining the value of automatic emails that feature new homes on the market. Steer clear of linking to canned pages about first time home buying, mortgages, or calculators.

Supply a page of your current listing pipeline for buyers and sellers to browse. Sellers are savvy today and will check out websites for functionality and listing exposure before deciding on an agent to market their home. Chances are they've purchased their own home after researching online first and know that other buyers will do the same. Unlike in traditional real estate trade papers, you have full

BRANDING

control of how you display your own listings. You can feature your personal listings with more detail, pictures, tours, and information.

Keep your home page simple so people can find what they want quickly. Easy navigation is essential to your success. There are a thousand bells and whistles you can add to your site, but resist the temptation. Too many extra items and effects can actually make your site look amateurish and will cause your page to load slowly. If your site takes too long to load information, prospects will move on to some other site.

The number one thing people want to do on your real estate site is search. Potential buyers simply want to view houses. With this in mind, you must build your site around a complete and easy to use IDX property search engine. IDX mapping features will show current listing locations with small icons that can be expanded for more information. Prospects can zoom in to see details about all of the current listings in their preferred area Clients can't ask for much more when surfing the Web for a new home.

A site has to be current to be relevant. All sites give you the ability to easily update your site with new content and listing info, but you have to put in the effort. When you get busy, your updates can fall off and before you know what's happened, your very attractive website is very out of date. Choose or design

INTERNET MARKETING

a website that fits your update and maintenance ability.

Your website will help you collect contact information and generate leads. A niche targeted and user friendly site with plenty of helpful information makes prospects feel comfortable enough to fill out a form with their information requesting further information. They may request email updates of new listings as they hit the market. They may ask for more information on a listing they found through searching your IDX engine. Prospects may subscribe to your E-newsletter, or ask a question about schools or the area. Most realtor boards offer MLS prospecting tools that automatically email prospects about new listings. If your board doesn't offer these tools, you can subscribe to a third party solution such as Housevalues.com. Keep everything simple and request only basic contact information like name, email address, and phone number. Include a disclaimer that you keep all information private, and do that. Privacy protection will reinforce your role as a professional who keeps his clients' best interests in mind.

Respond to inquiries as quickly as possible. Most people expect almost immediate responses. You can't wait until the next day to respond; you will lose the prospect. Set your cell phone to alert you of new emails so you can reply right away. Today's prospects are accustomed to getting a response within two hours, so get that Blackberry and make sure you are well connected.

Statistically, online real estate consumers are not very loyal. Only 23% of those who start their search online actually end up getting further live assistance from an agent whose site they have used on the Internet. Even worse, according to NAR only 7% of those prospects actually complete a transaction with an agent they've found online. This data tells us a few key pieces of information. First, there is great opportunity to brand yourself as the target market expert and capitalize on a niche centric site, because other sites will be too general. Second, better web skills are needed to maintain prospect relationships. Third, we are reminded of the importance of hitting the streets to network and make real world connections. Most buyers see the Internet as a source to gather information, but not as a source to find an agent or complete a real estate transaction. You can't change that perception, but with the right site, strategy, and skills you can improve your online lead- capture rate substantially.

Website marketing extends well beyond your personal website. Listing sites like Realtor.com, Homes.com, or your own company's corporate site provide you with administrative tools for page customization. Do not settle for the default design in any of these forums. As in the real world, all customizable online opportunities should be designed to reflect your brand image and message exactly.

The Web intimidates the herd. Instead of learning the easily available programs and tools, the herd attempts to employ canned, unoriginal sites that perpetuate their rank as dismal herd members. The herd's fear of the web makes them easy targets for those web site companies that promise all the goodies but deliver a site that looks like a million others. There are an unlimited amount of companies out there ready to offer you a cheap template. Most are ineffective and limit the ability to manipulate the design, function, and appearance of your website.

The herd also fears that websites are taking over and will reduce their role to simply transaction processors, kept in the deals only to do the paperwork. Branded agents know that providing information is a critical part of negotiation and the contract-to-close process. Web sites can actually be the beginning piece in creating life-long clients.

Even if a buyer who uses your site as a resource doesn't close a deal with you, he or she will remember your brand as being a vital resource. The time that buyer spent on your site didn't cost you any more time or money, but it was still instrumental in strengthening your brand. Brand growth comes one impression at a time. Visitors will recommend your site to others, further extending brand reach. Your website is a branding tool that gives you total control and operates with 24/7 target market exposure. To highlight your web presence to future clients, use your website both on a laptop and in quality print presentations as part of your pre-listing package and listing presentations.

Like any branding channel, you get what you pay for in time, commitment, and money. Good agent web sites can range in cost. You can choose from a wide range, including inexpensive customizable templates to full-blown professionally customized sites. The tendency is to just jump in headfirst, but you will be far more successful if you take the time to do your research.

Blogging, E-newsletters, and Social Networking

Blogging has become a window into the hearts and minds of online personas. Real estate blogging can further your brand's approachability and expose clients to your personality. People love discovering that there is more to an agent than just making sales. A blog needs to speak to your target market about your brand message and the services you provide. Simple strategies, like providing links to your site and newsletter, are crucial.

Also, some of your personal blogs will become the basis for newsletter stories and press releases. Remember to share stories, articles, news, and ideas in both your blog and your newsletters. To stretch the reach of your brand, you can repackage your blogs and submit them as articles through submission engines to any number of relevant news outlets and information sites. Articles are also another great inexpensive way to tell your brand story to those searching for information about your target market.

E-newsletters are another way to repackage information from your blogs, articles, and direct mail newsletters. They offer great opportunities to compel prospects to register to receive more information. Each communication lessens the barriers to future interaction, and people appreciate when others add value to their lives. That gratitude opens the doors to referral relationships. Similar to your off line newsletter, your E-newsletter may get very little attention before being deleted, but provides another non-invasive branded reminder that you are an expert working hard at the real estate business.

Social online networking provides a venue to exchange information and share ideas. These networks build on the growing reliance of online communication. Networks quickly help people connect and find the answers that were previously impossible to locate. Social networking is still developing. Get in early and stake claim your target market on line by providing resources and information to those seeking assistance.

Search Engines

Rule number one with websites is that they must be easily located. The most beautiful, functional, informative, and compelling site is not worth a dime if no one knows to visit. Putting your web address on all of your print materials is a start. Generally, people are used to visiting web sites for a deeper, more interactive look at products and services. Computers are now prevalent enough in everyone's lives that people "get it" and know they can plug in an address and get high definition photos, virtual tours, and information without speaking to anyone.

Most web users use one of the top two search engines to find what they want. Statistically, the consumers visit only the top listed sites when trying to find information. So the goal is to have your site listed first by these search engines when a prospect types in search terms relative to your target market. The process website creators have developed to maintain high search rankings is called search engine optimization.

House hunters conduct real estate searches based on area, lifestyle, price range, school districts, proximity to work, and a plethora of other criteria that they deem relevant in determining the location of their home. Potential buyers will enter the name of a geographic area and/or a lifestyle followed by "homes" or "real estate." "Greenville real estate," or "Aspen lakefront homes" are two typical search examples. Then the prospect would click on any of the top listed sites and decide within seconds whether to stay or hit the back button. If you are not high in search engine rankings, you might as well not be there at all, because your prospects won't find you any other way.

Yahoo and Google supply over 90% of the web's search results. The results are ranked by relevance according to certain proprietary ranking algorithms. Thousands of companies claim to know the secret of search ranking, but the criteria are still a closely guarded secret. For a small fee—but certainly no guarantee—these companies offer to move you up on the list by editing and adding ingredients like meta-tags, HTML add-ons, reciprocal and one way links, and a myriad of other edits to your website.

There are some reliable ways to optimize your website. For example, including articles on your site with a high percentage of pertinent keywords will help move your site up on the search list. All programmers agree that search engines look for content, so be sure you are including relevant, legitimate, targeted material. If you hide pages with nothing but keywords or repetitive material, the search engines will throw out your site as spam. You should write your own keyword heavy articles, blogs, and newsletters and place them on your site. There are also several search engine optimization sites that will syndicate your articles around the web creating reciprocal links to your site and further increase your search engine ranking.

Inherent in your brand is the advantage of having a specialized target market. A specific website will have much less competition fighting for the top spot. Clients are looking for specific search results, so even if a generalist in the herd has configured his site to rank high on the search results list, an interested prospect will choose your site. Searchers can differentiate between a general site and a specialized site immediately. Like any brand channel, search engine success takes time, work, and consistency. Eventually, you will get your site well ranked.

While experimenting to find your branded search engine top spot, try the pay per click listing features on Yahoo and Google. Pay per click is an online program owned by the respective search engines that allows you to bid on certain search terms. Your ranking is shown as a sponsored site alongside the natural search results. The rank is assigned based on how much competing websites are willing to pay each time a prospect clicks to visit their site. The higher the bid for a keyword or search term, the higher the sponsored search is ranked. Again the payoff is in specialization. While the herd bids up general search terms and keywords to as much as a few dollars a click, branded agents pay much less (as low as ten cents) for more specialized search terms that match their target market.

Most web surfers find pay per click results attractive, because if a company or individual is willing to pay to have someone visit a site, the creator must be confident that the site offers compelling value. Pay per click programs also provide you valuable tools and information about keywords, search terms, headers, and descriptions that increase your click through rates. Most companies provide you with an administrative site to keep track of your per click data and offer everything from detailed reports to search term suggestions.

Email

The email evolution has changed the way realtors provide their services. In the past, agents needed days and weeks to complete certain communications. But now agents can quickly deliver documents, contracts, addendums, listing pictures, videos, and data at a moments notice.

On one hand, email has given us a non-intrusive way to get our communication delivered. On the other hand, electronic communication has limited the ability to develop and maintain the personal relationships so vital to continued success. That's something you must keep in mind—do not work on a strictly email basis. E-blasts to other realtors are a great way to make your new listings known, and your sellers love the extra effort. Constant Contact is a great company to handle your broadcast logistics. Broadcast emails are good for general announcements and sending news to clients. But they are too impersonal to create the dependable relationships your clients deserve. Clients want your undivided attention and care. Broadcast or drip email campaigns may look like a great way to stay in front of clients, but be wary of substituting automatic client contact for the real thing. Clients realize the difference and often see broadcast emails as annoying spam. Although the info you send might be useful, people know they've been automatically tickled and don't view the email as a meaningful effort. Email campaigns are only best when lightly mixed with a heavy campaign of personal client contact and service.

Instead of using a tickler to automatically fire off a campaign of biweekly canned emails, use a tickler to remind you to send each client a personalized note. Branding with email is about being non–intrusive, while still making the point that your relationship with the recipient is paramount. You can do that with meaningful, concise writing and relevant information.

By now you know that even your email should be branded in style, design, and name. If you have your own website, you should be able to create your own email at your web address, such as Joe@pleasantvilleliving.com or Joe@joesmithrealty.com. Doing this will not only brand your email, but it will reinforce both your website and brand message.

The style of your email should be customized in some form, but try to keep branding to a simple header or signature. Steer clear of overdoing the email branding. Be careful when using stationary backgrounds; don't use big frames or frilly borders, even if that is part of your brand look. People want to be able to quickly scan the text of an email and move on. Email stationary that is too busy is unprofessional and can be stopped by virus software that flags your frills as dangerous attachments. Set up a tasteful and simple custom signature or header with your name, company, phone numbers, and links to your website. Once again, less is more. Instead of a signature at the bottom, you can include your brand header along with your branded photo, logo, and tagline. There are several programs and sites that customize headers and signatures. These layouts provide simple but compelling information that helps people find out more about your brand.

A great addition to your email is a v-card. A v-card is an industry standard electronic business card automatically used by most major database programs. Attaching your v-card to your email will automatically send all of your information to recipients who click on the graphic. Their system easily downloads all of your contact information directly into their address book.

Email capabilities will continue to evolve and improve the way agents serve their prospects and clients. Keeping up with email advancements can only help strengthen your brand. Remember that email will always be just a tool and never a substitute for good personal interaction.

BRANDING

Over the last two decades, the Internet has been a great way to set agents apart from their competition. But now electronic communication and advertising have become a routine part of the real estate services mix. As a result, there are increasing numbers of online companies, programs, and platforms offering searchable listing solutions, which further eclipses the agents' market influence. Large Internet companies will continue to gobble up what realtors once held as proprietary information. With so much competition, realtors have to specialize to gain market share. Branded agents are specialists by design. People will increasingly use the Internet to find data they once needed a realtor to find, but they will also increasingly use the Web to find a branded specialist to put the deal together.

Your internet plan is simple. Create a targeted and compelling site that mirrors your brand. Attract attention, incoming links, and prospects through blogs, articles, E-newsletters, and an aggressive SEO strategy. Use email to foster the relationships that you cultivate and fortify offline. With consistency you will have defined your branded niche in cyberspace. As in each of the seven brand channels, there are thousands of companies, applications, and programs that give promise to provide more leads to real estate agents. None are as effective in harnessing your online success as the few strategies we've discussed.

Chapter 11

Public Relations

Public relations can be defined as earning third party testimonials that position you as a respected expert in your field. In other words, this is a recommendation just as powerful as a personal referral. Publicity is a good thing, and there are steps in becoming a reliable resource for the writers, producers, and journalists in your market. PR is generally "free," but good PR takes a systematic approach.

A good brand exploits the media's need for news to shape brand identity and credibility. Good PR is akin to earning a third party testimonial for your brand expertise. For good or bad, most readers trust the opinion of the press. If the press quotes or references an agent, consumers will assume that agent is a respected and proven authority.

Additionally, many people like to be associated with the agent whom they see in the newspaper or on TV. Anything that gives your clients another way to impress their friends is a good way to strengthen your consumer loyalty. Whenever you are mentioned or interviewed regularly, you will experience some celebrity, and even a tiny bit of fame can really strengthen your brand image. Unlike the slow but powerful build of the other seven brand channels, PR provides a quick shot of elevated brand positioning.

The herd doesn't work to develop Public Relations because they don't think they are news-worthy. Branded agents *make* themselves newsworthy. The bottom line is that every publication, news production, and media outlet has to fill space and time. They are hungry for good filler. Real estate is a business that deals with lifestyles, people, and places, and therefore provides plenty of relevant stories, news, and information of interest to the public. And with the herd out of the way, PR is a wide-open opportunity for the strategically prepared brand.

Writers, producers, and journalists always have strict deadlines. They need complete stories immediately, which can work to your advantage. You will be amazed at the coverage you get from simply submitting press releases about your important activities. Work on creating win-win situations for both you and the journalist. Providing brand centric but newsworthy stories of interest will get your name on print and screen. The key is to provide information within the required timeline and in the correct format.

Make a journalist's job easier, and you will get the press. Always be accessible, professional, and quick to return calls when working with members of the media. When you don't return phone calls or are hard to reach, writers will opt to work with someone else. Providing the best story at the right time may take frequent submissions, but eventually your release will be the perfect fit. Positive PR pays off more than paid advertising because consumers view the news as much more credible than advertising, and it doesn't cost you a dime.

Journalists rely on quotable experts to make their articles more objective and trustworthy. They want informative and defining statements to lend credibility to their reports. The more you can add articulate, concise, and compelling quotes about a subject, the more you will be mentioned in the media. So prepare your comments before being interviewed. If you can position yourself as a cooperative, reliable source that responds quickly, you can become the branded real estate resource of choice for your targeted media sources.

Parlaying your coverage into being an expert source just takes networking, time, and effort. To be successful, you need to know the players, master press release logistics, and create a branded PR kit.

Press Releases

Formulate a press release with newsworthy information that will appeal to your customer base and to the media source's readers. There are many events in your life and business that will interest the general public. Hosting an event, creating an innovative process, leading a charity group, or winning an award all warrant press. The problem is that no one will know unless you share the information.

With a press release you are giving your media contacts a "heads up" on newsworthy information that will interest their readers. Gather recent market data and explain the current trends in your area. Believe it or not, people find the real estate industry very interesting. For most, their home is their biggest investment, and anything that affects their property value is relevant. Release information about anything that can be covered from a real estate angle. Don't be shy about putting out releases about awards you've won, accolades you've received, and certifications and designations you've earned. Listed in the press, these achievements carry a lot more weight, and you won't appear to be blowing your own horn. Look for opportunities that give you a unique professional angle, and you'll have plenty of releases accepted for publication.

Journalists are very busy, and although you may think you have an incredible story, you still need to follow their submission rules to be considered. Follow these steps to writing a press release, and your submission will stand out from the pile:

Give release date instructions. Write your instructions clearly at the top of the page. "For immediate Release" is the best choice if your release isn't time sensitive, but you can also use, "For Release after [date]."

Prepare a compelling headline. Your headline should answer the question: "Why would this interest people?"

Begin with a brief description of your news. You should entice the reader with a short teaser, and then follow with your personal information.

Be concise. Producers and writers have a limited amount of time. They won't be willing or able to sift through several releases a day. Grab their attention early and limit your release to a page or less if possible. Begin with the facts, avoid excessive use of adjectives, keep your audience in mind, and get to the point.

Provide all significant details. Answer the questions "who, what, when, where, why, and how" in the first paragraph if possible. Leaving out specific details won't make your contacts want to pick up the phone and call you; they will only be frustrated that you didn't complete the job.

Supply all important contact information. Include contact names, address, phone numbers, email, fax number, and website if relevant. Make sure you include the best hours to reach you.

End your release. This seems simple enough, but by ending your release with the word "end" or "###," you make organization easier for the journalist who may have piles of research, releases, and other documents to read.

Press Kit

Introduce yourself to the key people at each of the appropriately targeted media outlets. Do this by creating a press kit or introductory package about you and your brand. This alone will set you apart from the other agents who may also be rallying for the local expert spot. This is your first impression, so package your press kit professionally and in an orderly manner. Remember to create plenty of extra copies so you have several on hand. The following items will create a cohesive press kit that will help you stand out from the rest.

Personal Photo – Include printed and digital copies of a high quality black and white *and* full color branded photo. Include at least two different shots, because as you get more publicity the press will need different photo options.

References – Provide a page of references and testimonials from clients and networking associates. Name dropping here is not taboo, so if you have some clients who are well-known and in good standing in the community, request a testimonial from them to use in your kit and on the web.

PUBLIC RELATIONS

Press Release – Include a few non time-sensitive releases in the kit to compel the media to do a spotlight piece on you, the local market expert.

Articles and Newsletters – Submit articles, your newsletter, a branded printout of the site and your blog, and a few direct mail pieces. Recipients of your kit are used to the usual herd materials, so show them your brand is best.

Personal Brochure – Your personal brochure tells your brand story and conveys your brand message, and it should therefore be the centerpiece of your kit. The quality should be so impressive that people pass your brochure around the office.

Previous Media Coverage – Add a list or include copies of articles in which you've been quoted, referenced, or spotlighted. Listing your past media coverage ensures the press that you have already been a trusted and reliable source to other journalists.

Speaking Topics – Another way to create credibility is to list topics about which you are prepared to speak and provide brief descriptions of each.

FAQs – List common questions and answers that are relevant to your business and niche. This will make the journalist's job much easier and provides quick filler if ever needed.

BRANDING

In addition to giving your press kits to the media, send some to organizations as a proposal for speaking engagements or to open up discussion leading opportunities. Use your kit as an introductory tool for networking groups and associations that you would like to become involved with.

One quick word of caution: don't forget the reason you are looking for media exposure in the first place—to promote your brand. Some agents get caught up in the excitement of being on television or in the press and miss the opportunity to forge their brand identity. They end up appearing nervous or over-rehearsed. This is an opportunity to showcase your brand in a positive light, so prepare wisely. Remember that confidence and presentation are more than half the battle. Know the ramifications for any stance that you take on an issue, especially how your opinion will affect your target market. If you know your values and interests are in line with those of your target market, then you should be fine.

The press usually has an angle for any given story. Be careful that your support of their angle is aligned with your brand identity. Your target market can easily get confused or even offended if you publicly state the opposite of what you are known to believe. Prepare for press interviews like you would a listing appointment. Articulate your position, which should be consistent with your stance in press releases, press kit materials, and other quotes provided to the media.

After people see you and read about you in the press, they will seek your advice, trust your opinion, and request your guidance more often. This priceless brand positioning may be hard work, but it is inexpensive and offers endless and unparalleled exposure opportunities. Whether you are quoted or simply mentioned in the media, the impact is impressive and memorable.

Chapter 12

Personal Brochure

The agent Personal Brochure is an opportunity to provide focused copy that tells the story of your brand. The goal is to hook your target with a high quality piece that celebrates your unique and honest brand and position you as a unique but relevant expert. Your style and standards are displayed to help readers evaluate your professionalism. Your story serves to enhance positive emotional ties to your brand identity.

A brochure allows complete expression of brand identity in one single piece of advertising. Brand photos, colors, logos, taglines, style, design, and copy are all part of the brochure design. A brochure literally tells your brand story and should be combined with other brand channels as a networking tool, a direct mail piece, a downloadable file on your site, part of your press kit, and a piece of your listing and sales presentation packages.

Many agents know that there is value in the personal brochure, because the most successful agents utilize them. But many agents who try to employ the approach make one common mistake. They use the personal brochure as a showcase for a resume or list of achievements. Brochures with that kind of content do nothing to create interest or lay branding groundwork. People don't respond to you because you have reached volume benchmarks in your career; they want to work with you because you understand their needs and provide the benefits to make their lives better. Your personal brochure has to be about your unique story, the relevant benefits you offer as their expert, and the consistency that you employ in your marketing and services from contract to close.

Begin by writing as much as you can about your life and career. Use the notes you made during the "Discovering Your Brand" process. What were the lessons, hurdles, and tests that made you who you are? What do you value about your target market? The herd was taught to promote accomplishments and claim to be the best sellers, home finders, and relocation experts. But consumers want to know *what makes* an agent the best. Although your achievements may be impressive, only mention them subtly, as a *part* of your story. Talk about the type of realtor you are, and give examples. Speak about building relationships instead of pushing readers to use your services.

To people already familiar with your brand, the look and feel of your brochure will be enough to further solidify your position. To others, your brochure will be an introduction to your brand. You will need to create an intriguing brochure cover to get your reader interested in the contents. The front cover will determine whether the prospective client keeps reading or puts the brochure down. Whether your cover has a question, single word, phrase, or just a photo, the design should inspire the reader to keep reading. If you ask a provocative question, don't supply the answer on the cover; entice your readers to turn the page and find out. If you use the cover to advertise a long list of awards or skills, your readers will stop—they have heard this all before. Your brochure is not a hard sales letter, but an invitation to get to know you better.

Your brochure should also take an unconventional approach with cover graphics. For one thing, don't assume that you should start with a big picture of yourself on the cover. Keep your niche in mind. Open with a key phrase that relates to your niche, and then have a professional photo that communicates the same idea. And if you do use a photo of yourself on the cover, then by all means make sure the shot is a personable one that your audience can connect with. For example, if your niche is a family oriented community, you may want to use a photo of yourself teaching a child how to fish at the neighborhood lake. If your niche is Colorado Mountain living, you may want an action shot of you hiking in the majestic mountains with your dog. Remember you are selling yourself as a person who fits in with the niche, and you will be judged by the appearance of your photos. Use them as a chance to evoke the right warm feelings and to connect with your market.

A winning brochure is a big challenge. You will need the guidance of a professional copywriter and graphic designer. The copy should also be used on your website, and the design needs to be done in line with your brand look and style.

Make certain that whomever you choose to design your personal brochure is on board with the approach, style, and ideas that you wish to convey. Most graphic artists and designers are experienced in personal brochure production. Remember, this process is still slightly unconventional; your professional team needs to understand that this is just the opposite of the average agent's brochure. You'll want to hire someone who will work with you and understands your needs. Many brochure designers work off templates and can get confused when you come to them with something that they aren't used to doing. Ask to see samples of their work, discuss your ideas with them, and make sure you feel comfortable before making decisions. The upfront cost of copy and design will be a drop in the bucket compared to the impact and success that can be generated by a winning brochure. You can afford the expense; the first deal you put together will cover the cost.

A branded agent cannot afford to forego a branded personal brochure. If you need some help, the trade publication *Broker Agent Magazine* has proven to be one of the most effective all around personal brochure options available. If you have the visual aspects of your brand, photo, logo, tagline, colors, and a basic design, you can turn material over to the copywriters and printers at *Broker Agent.* You will get a sponsored feature spread in the publication, and may order copies of your article to use as your brochure. The cost of this method is a fraction of the fees charged by many of the large brochure design companies. Besides being a high quality publication, your brochure will have a vital third party testimonial component by having the magazine name across the header of the brochure. It is a quality approach that tells your brand story and comes across as a referral. There are many other options out there, but this is one that works well.

Your copy is best when written in the third person. Third person subtly removes implications of your own ego while still relating your story and successes. Third person also adds an air of truth, because the style reads like a traditional story. Being portrayed as positive and human in pictures and copy is your best shot at connecting emotionally with your target audience. Your story must make people feel comfortable enough to trust you. Your story creates familiarity. This is a lot to ask of a brochure, but is actually very possible with a little imagination and effort.

Once you have created a personal brochure that artfully captures the essence of your brand, put the brochure to work for you. There are numerous ways to use it to generate more leads and business. You can use your brochure as a prospecting tool to gain new clients and to create stronger relationships. Bring your personal brochure to open houses, leave copies at your listings, and send them in relocation kits. Use them to network at Chamber of Commerce events, share them with members of your sphere of influence, and have cooperating businesses keep a stack available for clients. Send brochures out to your client database and target market. Put them in your pre-listing package and provide them to attendees at events and meetings at which you will speak. Display your personal brochure at hotels, visitor centers, and your local Chamber of Commerce if possible. The objective is to familiarize your niche market with you in a non-threatening but effective way. As people continually see your brochure tool and recognize you as a quality person and professional, they will begin to feel like they know you. And just from that you will gain more business than you ever imagined. That's the power of branding.

You will have to work less to prove yourself, because your brochure provides a non-threatening sales approach. To some degree, you will have a pre-established relationship and will spend less time explaining your brand background and more time getting to know your client's exact needs. Branded agents know that success has never come from telling clients how great you are, but from having a relationship based on understanding and trust.

These 7 Brand Channels are the foundation of a successful brand. Your message and visual brand identity should be indistinguishable throughout each channel. Carefully crafted and developed now, your brand processes will make you the agent first in mind. Don't cut corners, or you'll continually need to repair your foundation when you should be listing and selling. If you set up each of the 7 Channels correctly from the beginning and follow through, you will become the branded realtor of choice in your target market.

You now have a method that will separate you from the pack for you as long as you continue to nourish your brand. There are so many options in both marketing and advertising that the herd gets paralyzed and falls back into doing the same few things that everyone else does. Don't let that happen just do these seven things and your real estate business will take off. You've built the perfect brand for the authentic You, Inc. Now make sure you continue to genuinely live the brand, so that your business can prosper in even the most adverse markets.

SECTION IV

Being Your Brand

You've discovered and built the brand that best suits your unique self and the market you have passionately chosen to serve. Your brand is beginning to make an impact and is positioning you as the realtor first in mind with your niche. Now that you've done all of the difficult upfront work, take a step back to make sure that your brand is sending the right message to your targeted audience.

Being your brand requires key fundamentals that will help you to portray a unique, relevant, and consistent brand life going forward. You must continually maintain the seven branding channels as working cogs in your real estate business. One ad, one mailer, one brochure, one email, or one introduction won't position you as the agent first in mind, but consistent effort on all of these fronts will. Now you just need to keep working the plan.

Branded agents completely understand the value of the standards and systems they employ both in and out of real estate. They use their knowledge to make organization and balance a part of their lives. These skills are vital to creating and keeping the relationships that enrich your life and your business. Implementing solid organized systems, consistent brand standards, unwavering life balance, and continual testing of your brand channels are the ongoing challenges of being your brand.

Chapter 13

Branded Systems

Successfully completing transactions from contract to closing requires systems. Organization, maintaining budgets, and implementation also call for systems. Branded systems determine the methods that you employ to do things, and the standards to which you do them. In your business, your systems are what allow you to effectively solve clients' problems, meet their needs, and manage everything else that arises. The right systems enable you to efficiently provide a customer experience that lives up to everything that your brand promises.

There are two goals when establishing systems in your branded business. The first goal is to create the most effective and efficient processes. The second is to establish the highest standards that you can consistently maintain within your budget and framework. When working within an established company, most of the systems and processes have already been established. Your best bet is to work with the real estate company's processes and adapt your own systems to the ones already is place. Use the company's systems and whatever useful tools that are available. Aligning with the established processes creates the flow and synergy needed to ensure satisfied clients. Efficient and effective alternative methods can always be suggested to managers but do so discreetly and with tact.

The most crucial real estate system to master is database management. Database management is the nerve center of your business. The difference between a contact and a client is the relationship that you foster. If handled correctly, your contacts will become relationships and referral sources that you will keep for the life of your business. Having a database of 2,000 names is not worth much unless you have systematically added value to each by creating real relationships. Your branding will help with the relationships, but you still need a solid database system to ensure all of the working aspects of your business are operating effectively.

Database management has effectively become one of the key systems in a successful brand presence. Good systems build trust in your brand. By using a program to handle your appointments, contacts, and correspondence you are enhancing your ability to create quality relationships. Database management software systems are still a relatively new phenomenon. Over the past twenty years they have revolutionized our real estate business. Optimizing scheduling capabilities creates brand opportunities.

BRANDED SYSTEMS

Finding contact information fast and keeping track of needs, requests, and promises creates brand identity. Quickly being able to respond with MLS info, transaction status, or contract information creates brand loyalty. Internet and email integration has enabled agents to dramatically increase the speed and depth of information they provide their clients.

Typically, the database management system that you use depends on your wiring. Some agents do very well with a structured day and prefer a rigid appointment schedule. Others do better within a casual environment and make the most of opportunities as they come. The herd uses contact databases as phone books. The branded agent constantly sorts the data into manageable categories of clients, for which he applies appropriate action plans. The herd is worried about the circle of concern—everyone they have met. For that reason, their databases lack focus and purpose. The branded agent starts with a small sphere of influence, a handful of essential people. These are the relationships that are individually nurtured to create lifelong loyal referral sources.

The right database management tool is the one that works best for you—not the easiest, but the most effective one. Most agents lack the discipline needed to find out what database management tools are right for them. Now is a good time to step out of your box and demo different planning systems. The one that will help you to be accountable to your clients and goals for the long term is the one best for you.

Other than database management you must master file flow systems within your business. File flow systems are everything you do to list and sell property and to get a buyer from pre-contract to post close. Much of your file flow process will depend on the company that you work for. Simple adjustments like having online access to listing and contract templates will save you time and travel. Master spreadsheets or tracking software that schedules important dates and duties will save you nightmares, and sometimes even the deal.

Some of these methods may not seem any better than keeping written records, but they do free up more time, time best used to grow your relationships and referrals. Systems tickle what branded piece is to be created, by whom, and flag the release date. Each step in a file flow system triggers the next step toward completion. When inspections are done, timelines for addendums are set. Once delivered, another timeline for response is set. Once cleared, the title can be finalized and so on. When you acquire a new listing, you must begin working on brochures, ads, and MLS input processes. The herd approaches these pieces of the real estate puzzle with a checklist. Branded agents approach with a computerized file flow system. The perception of your brand identity will be improved because of your efficiency.

BRANDED SYSTEMS

Defining your systems is not unlike taking inventory. Branding, file flow, and database management all have to be systematized through technology. Technology and processes are hard for many agents to really understand, because they have never taken the time to break down exactly what they are doing. The process begins with simply writing down everything you must do to provide your branded real estate services. The more efficient your actionable processes are, the more time you can spend strengthening relationships. The herd doesn't do this work, but your ability to bring these steps into focus enables you to be accountable and to set expectations. Implementing these steps enables you to set goals, prioritize tasks, and improve the process that provides your best standards of service.

File flow is tedious, but without a handle on conditions, contingencies, deadlines, and branding channels, you will fall back into the herd. Your clients will have low expectations and receive terrible service. Keeping abreast of real estate technology must be a priority, as real estate technology will always be a moving target. Whatever steps you have implemented for file flow today could be made obsolete by something new next year. Your flow systems will always be changing; you just need to make sure they always change for the better.

Chapter 14

Brand Standards

Once you have your systems in place and working for you, create brand standards for each and everything you do, and then stick to them. Your standards can be as simple as always being on time or providing a thoughtful closing gift or a hand written thank you note. Whatever standards you set for your brand, keep in mind that these are the things that, once established, will set you apart from the herd and will create an expectation that you must live up to each and every time.

Something as simple as your standard for preparing and delivering a listing appointment is a process that can distance you from the herd. According to NAR, 67% of people talk to only one realtor, so getting the appointment is the hard part. For the 33% of deals that require you work a little harder, nothing should be left to chance. Don't be over-scripted, because that makes you appear manipulative. Listing and sales scripts also diminish your listening skills.

Create a thoughtful, chronological approach to your listing presentation that gives you the latitude to guide the appointment. But more importantly your presentation should have room for you to listen a great deal. A prelisting package delivered before your appointment is a great way to set you apart. The materials should include branded pieces like your brochure, testimonials, and marketing examples. Create standards like this for every aspect of your business, and you will improve your brand identity every step of the way.

How you present contracts and addendums throughout the process, whether mailed, emailed, or delivered, speaks to your commitment and to your branding. Client expectations never stop. There is no grace period, and there are no exceptions. The rare occasions when a client might overlook poor photography or cheap materials are the opportunities to make your branding systems and standards shine even brighter. You should approach things like meetings, presentations, offers, contingencies, commitments, settlements, etc. with consistent steps and standards. Consistent standards set client expectations and ensure proper delivery of services. If your MLS printouts have a color scheme that differs from that of your brand, are printed on cheap paper, or are delivered from a different email address, then you are falling short of your branding standards. Change your MLS templates to match that of You, Inc., and give them the same branded look as everything else you do.

If you take more than an hour to respond to an email today, then you are probably missing a branding opportunity. If your email header and signature don't reflect your brand or supply all of your contact information, then your standards aren't set to take advantage of another big branding opportunity. If you don't mail out weekly listing updates, or if they don't reflect your brand image, not only are you missing a branding opportunity, but you are compromising the concerted branding effort your 7 Channels have made along the way. All services, information, or material that is output from your systems and flow must reflect your brand.

Your brand standards create a competent and professional perception of your brand. The herd claims to employ these attention to detail service benefits, but they aren't consistent and do not register with the clients. Whether you are working on the contract, the appraisal, the inspection, or the closing, there are always opportunities to brand and shine. Nothing brands you more than a job well done.

Your ability to handle negotiations, contract issues, ethical procedures, and a myriad of other issues is part of your consistent standards. Much of your success in these situations is dependant on your technical skills and knowledge of the business. Good real estate knowledge is a must. Ongoing education provides you with a better understanding of the business and prepares you for logistic success. Knowledge makes you better equipped to handle situations and to offer the best service. Your standards of competency depend on continuing education, certifications, and designations that make you a smarter agent. Make continuing education one of your brand standards. Never stop learning, so that you can best serve your clients.

The best brand standards under-promise and over-deliver. Accept responsibility for whatever happens and fix situations that go wrong—this is what consumers expect of experts with integrity. The herd thinks clients will understand problems—they don't. Clients expect things to work perfectly, and they expect you to not make mistakes with their money. If you have a staff, make sure they are on board with all of your standards, especially those dealing with customer service. *You* are the brand, so anyone who represents your business must have You, Inc. in mind.

Life Balance

The path to real estate success is strewn with the burned out careers of agents who tried to succeed through the use of cold calling, scripts, and gimmicks. Many more agents got out of the business, because they neglected their own health, emotional, or even spiritual needs while trying to sell real estate. A balanced life and career stems from constantly addressing the emotional, mental, spiritual, and physical needs that all of us have.

Nourishing your heart, body, mind, and soul always leads to a full life with less stress and more joy. Balance in any business is crucial to long-term success. The price of not living a balanced life is unhappiness, illness, self-sabotage, loneliness, depression, etc. That's just a fact of life. Bad habits and living patterns are hard to break and many times even harder to acknowledge. Unfortunately, others can easily see when your life is out of balance, and there are countless ways that a life out of balance will detrimentally affect your brand.

People respect those who take care of themselves. Always begin with yourself. Take care of your mental, physical, emotional, and spiritual needs first, to put you in the best position to take care of others. Whether they realize this fact or not, branded agents maintain balance by meeting their personal needs. They are spiritual in their own personal ways. Aligning in spirit, whichever method they use, brings them peace in the tough times and enables them to remain grateful and giving. Mentally, branded agents keep everything simple. They stay sharp reading literature that enhances their lives, taking real estate courses, and pursuing all the interests that they have in common with their chosen target market. By staying mentally fit, branded agents offer better negotiating skills, craft better transactions, and best articulate benefits and solutions.

Staying physically healthy is a lifestyle. Unfortunately, most people let their health slide before anything else in their lives. That should be the last thing you neglect. There is no sense in becoming a great brand, if you become unhealthy on your way to the top. Whether you choose to hike, swim, lift weights, or practice yoga, exercise is vital to your brand's strength. By showing others that you take the time care for yourself, you immediately convey that you are very capable of taking care of them. Having the self-discipline to eat right and exercise will help create the time and space for everything else your brand work requires.

Branded agents feel good, maintain high self-confidence, and leave no room for depression and apathy. Good health sets the stage for emotional well-being. Your emotional needs like love, peace, and fulfillment should not be neglected so you can spend more time in the office, either. Like a steam engine, when the pressure becomes too great, you will blow. Being peaceful and fulfilled and having love in your life is what keeps your engine tuned and running. Branding is a process—a marathon, not a sprint. There should always be plenty of time given to love, life, and laughter. Success comes from being the agent first in mind. Fulfillment comes from the greater good that you decide to serve with your real estate knowledge and financial success. Peace and happiness come from the relationships you have along your journey.

Chapter 15

Brand Testing

When creating a successful brand, keep a close watch on the way your brand is perceived by your target audience. After all, they are the true judge and jury of your brand. With that said, so many aspects of your brand are left up to personal interpretation, which makes testing the effectiveness difficult. Because of this, your brand testing should consist of three ongoing steps: listen, ask, and track.

As a branded agent you are already involved within your niche. You know them, understand them, and are in tune with the happenings around town. As your brand develops, pay close attention to the way you are treated, and monitor any drastic changes that you notice. Take note of compliments, criticisms, and feedback that you receive. Is everything in line with your brand standards and identity? If not, make corrections to steer your brand in the right direction. You must continue to listen to the public, whether you are just beginning your brand creation, or have been a successful brand for decades. Perception is king, and if you are unaware of negative opinions about your brand because you didn't take time to listen, you could have disastrous results.

As you get feedback of any kind, learn as much as possible about the perception of your brand by engaging the source and asking for more information. For example, if a client tells you that you were the best agent he ever worked with, ask how this experience was different from previous experiences and what specifically was satisfying about your services. Clarifying can give you priceless insight and can help you make any changes that are needed.

If you are not comfortable asking for feedback in person, you can send out surveys to test your brand's presence. Give them to all clients, presentation attendees, and anyone else whom you work with closely. For example, send the survey to members of your business association. For the most informative results, make sure the survey asks open ended questions.

Make sure you have a system in place for those channels such as advertising, internet and direct mail that allow for physical tracking of results. In all of these cases, you have a financial investment at stake, so knowing how effective your advertising has been is crucial. Not all of these channels should be judged strictly by the numbers, because most of your marketing is meant to brand you and not necessarily to directly drive sales. Either way, monitor all of your advertising and marketing so that by the end of the year you will have a good idea where to invest and what to avoid.

Strengthening your brand through solid organized systems, consistent brand standards, unwavering life balance, and continuous testing of your brand channels will only allow for your brand to grow and prosper more quickly. These fundamentals operate as the checks and balances needed to ensure success now and in the future. Put these processes in place and nourish them now while you have the time to focus on their importance.

Brand Commandments

The new brand that you've labored to discover and build will reward you with further opportunities for a balanced life and a prosperous business. As you nourish your brand both now and in the future keep the following Brand Commandments at the forefront of every decision, change, and thought. With each element I have included a series of self assessment questions you can use to reevaluate your brand. Use them for guidance anytime you need reassurance or reinforcement:

Consistency.

- Does your brand represent a consistent singular brand message through each and every one of the 7 Brand Channels?

- Is your look and style consistent in every material that you create or send?
- Are your brand standards in place and implemented consistently in everything that you do?
- Is everyone that works on your brand on board with the standards and vision of your brand?
- Is the feedback that you receive consistent with the brand that you represent?

Quality.

- Are you exemplifying the personal integrity upon which your brand is built?
- Is the client experience of the quality that your brand promises?
- Are you doing all that you can to ensure quality in all aspects of your business?
- Are your physical materials of the quality that is expected of your brand?

Authenticity.

- Are you remaining true to your brand in every way possible?
- Does your brand continue to be relevant to the niche that you serve?
- Is your brand still aligned with your true self?
- Is the life that you are living and the perception of your brand one in harmony?

- Do you genuinely enjoy your brand and your niche?
- Are you living the life that you were meant to live?
- Do you have balance between your business and the things that you care about most?

Accessibility.

- Are you mentally and physically available to your brand and accessible to your target market?
- Are you committed to designating time to continually live and interact within your niche?
- Are you the same personable brand that brought you success in the first place?
- Are you maintaining the little things that are so important in growing and sustaining a brand, such as making yourself available and engaging those within your niche?

Reinvesting.

- Are you continuing to reinvest in your brand?
- Are you putting a minimum of 15% of your gross income back into promoting and developing your brand further?
- Are you adjusting your investment as your income level adjusts?

- Do you continue to adapt your brand's promotional and marketing opportunities towards new and relevant opportunities?
- Do you continue to reinvest the energy that you get from your brand's success into your niche community?

These are the commandments that you must live by and the questions you must answer to make sure you are living and working to your best potential. Whether you are just beginning the process of creating your brand or have been working long term, these commandments will guide you to stay true to your brand and standards. Always be aware of changes you may need to make. Live your brand with an open awareness, and you will always be ready for the next move. Many in the herd make the mistake of not seeing their brand through once they've put the work into the creation. You have to be present to truly know your brand and understand its needs.

Conclusion

This whole process may seem tedious, but in the end the reward is worth every single second of work you put into your brand. Be proud of your brand—you've done the hard work that most people skip, and an authentic brand is the result. Know that every time you promote your brand, go on a listing appointment, or network at an event, the brand you represent is meaningful and honest. Be proud that you have the courage and integrity to conduct your business the right way. You've let your consumers in and have opened yourself up for great success that will only get better as more people realize that you are the real deal.

The power of branding is something that will affect your business almost instantly and continue to surprise you as you nurture your brand with great care. You'll experience outstanding earnings, more quality time with your family, and a career that you'll enjoy more than you ever could have imagined. You may have the opportunity to work with the most influential leaders in your community. You may even be considered a significant leader yourself, and one who is regarded as the expert in your field. Publicity will come easily to you. You'll develop a great reputation and get leads from people that you've never even met. Branding has the power to make a community believe that they know you, and can relate to, and trust you. Branding will change your life.

As with any new process, you may be both excited and a little nervous to make such a strong commitment to change. Any deviation from a familiar path will always be a little daunting. Experiencing some anxiety is normal. Every successful person has moments of doubt when beginning a new career, trying a new process, or making a life altering change. But looking back now, most would honestly say that taking that first step to a new life and career was the best decision that they've ever made. You have to start somewhere. You can't live on the fence forever, especially if you want to realize your dreams. If you are too intimidated to put everything that you have into creating a powerful personal brand, you will never realize the power and potential that you are so capable of – and that may be the biggest mistake of your life.

Life and business are always better if you stand for something, and with your brand you now have the confidence to know that, with everything you do, you represent the best of yourself. You may win some deals and lose others, but you'll never spend sleepless nights worrying that you are a fraud. You

CONCLUSION

and your beliefs are there on the table for consumers to examine. If they don't choose to work with you, they probably aren't the type of clients that you want. Those that do have the opportunity to work with you will bring you great personal joy and endless business, because you have conducted yourself in a professional and honest light. You are authentic in all that you do, and because of that, you enjoy your life, your business, your family, and your freedom. Isn't that what all of your hard work is about?

Branding:

The Real Estate Agent Workbook

Welcome to ***Branding: The Real Estate Agent Workbook.*** Like many of your colleagues, you may have decided that your real estate career needs a jump start. Congratulations- you've come to the right place. The unique approach to marketing discussed in this course has been carefully developed and tested by professionals, and will change the way you approach your business forever.

Branding isn't just about creating a recognizable image for your real estate business. The process begins with in-depth self evaluation, assessment of personal values, and a search for your authentic self. This workbook has been designed to complement the information you will receive in our branding workshop, as well to help you prepare for your own adventure in branding.

Self-Analysis

Your passions

13. What are you passionate about?

___

14. What would you do every day if you didn't need to work?

___

15. If you could pick only one activity to do for the rest of your life, what would it be?

___

Considering your answers:

Start researching the organizations and groups that are associated with your favorite activities and interests.

> Where do the members of these groups live, work, and play?
>
> _____
> _____
> _____
> _____
> _____
> _____
>
> What other things do they enjoy?
>
> _____
> _____
> _____
> _____
> _____
> _____

Your qualities

16. What is unique about you?

17. What is your most distinct personal characteristic?

18. What do you get most compliments on?

Remember, most people enjoy working with agents that they can relate to. Finding a place for your unique mannerisms, characteristics, and quirks in your brand is important because they are critical to your authenticity and appeal.

Your skills

19. What is your greatest strength?

_____

20. What is unique about your services?

_____

21. What do you do that adds a distinctive value?

_____

BRANDING

On the lines below, make note of any specific praise or comments that you consistently receive from satisfied clients, managers, and coworkers.

_____
_____
_____
_____
_____
_____
_____
_____

Do you notice any common themes? This exercise is important to recognize aspects of your business that matter to your clients. These are you're your natural talents and skills that will enhance your brand and should be highlighted.

List common themes here:

_____
_____
_____
_____
_____
_____
_____

Your values

22. What are you most proud of?

_____
_____
_____
_____
_____

23. What do you want to be known for?

_____
_____
_____
_____
_____

Your values represent who you are at the core, and they will be the nucleus of your personal brand. The purpose of this exercise is to discover your true authentic self and resolve any conflicts between what you think you are projecting and what you actually *are* projecting.

Discovering Your Niche

Passions

What things or activities do you love the most? What are you most passionate about in life?

_____
_____
_____
_____

After considering your passions, can you dial in specifically on what you like or enjoy most about it (them)?

_____
_____
_____
_____

Make a list of the places you can find information about your niche and the people who live in it:

_____
_____
_____
_____
_____

Aligning Your Image and Style

Do you fit into the specialty or target market you have chosen?

- Yes, absolutely. This niche fits my personality, lifestyle, and values perfectly.

- Somewhat, I need to refine my focus. With some adjustments to my brand or to the niche, this could work. (Use the lines below to describe the changes you might make.)

  _____
  _____
  _____
  _____
  _____
  _____

- Not at all. I would be compromising my personal lifestyle, values, and or authentic self to fit into this market.

BRANDING

Target Market Analysis Example

Use the following three step formula to determine if your chosen target market can support your business. The final number reflects the number of homes you would need to sell to sustain your business and reach your goals.

1. Average Home Price × Average Commission = Average Commission

    $300,000 × 3% = $9000

2. Income Goal ÷ Average Commission = Transaction Goal

    $200,000 ÷ $9000 = 22.2 Homes
    Just under 2 homes a month

3. 2 × Transaction Goal ÷ Turnover Rate = Minimum # of Homes per Niche needed to succeed

    a. 2 × 22.2 (transaction goal) = 44.4

    b. 44.4 ÷ .04 = 1110 Homes

This formula doesn't account for any brokerage splits, but you can figure in your split by taking the average commission and multiplying that by your share.

Target Market Analysis Worksheet

Use the following worksheet with your actual data to determine if your niche market is large enough to support your business.

1. Average Home Price × Average Commission = Average Commission

   $_____ × __%__ = $_____

2. Income Goal ÷ Average Commission = Transaction Goal

   $_____ ÷ $_____ = ____ Homes

3. 2 × Transaction Goal ÷ Turnover Rate = Minimum # of Homes per Niche

   a. 2 × ____ (transaction goal) = _____

   b. . ÷ ____ = ____ Homes

Exploring Your Niche

Understanding your niche market will guide you to always best make the right marketing decisions for your brand. Create a blueprint of your market by using your niche research to complete this worksheet. Keep your findings in mind to build and maintain a consistent and laser focused brand.

Target Market Likes:

_____
_____
_____
_____
_____

Target Market Dislikes:

_____
_____
_____
_____
_____

Important Target Market Issues:

_____
_____
_____
_____
_____

Hot Target Market Topics:

_____
_____
_____
_____
_____

Target Market Activities:

_____
_____
_____
_____
_____

BRANDING

Target Market Style:

Target Market Preferred Recreation:

Target Market Preferred Schools and Colleges:

Target Market Hotspots:

Target Market Organizations:

Target Market Popular Events:

BRANDING

Target Market Preferred Affiliations, Associations, and Clubs:

_____
_____
_____
_____
_____

Target Market Preferred Publications:

_____
_____
_____
_____
_____

Target Market Qualities:

_____
_____
_____
_____
_____

Target Market Skills:

Target Market Values:

Target Market Lifestyle:

BRANDING

Target Market Demographics:

_____
_____
_____
_____
_____

Target Market Preferred Charitable Organizations:

_____
_____
_____
_____
_____

Other:

_____
_____
_____

Building Your Brand

Photos:

Use your photo to make a connection with your target market. List some possible photo ideas that will best relate you to your target market:

Poses:

_____
_____
_____
_____
_____

Locations:

_____
_____
_____
_____
_____

Wardrobe:

_____
_____
_____
_____
_____

Logos

A successful logo must:

1. Apply basic design fundamentals
2. Represent your brand message
3. Function across different media
4. Create a memorable impression

List logos of other companies that are memorable to you:

_____
_____
_____
_____

Why do these logos stand out to you?

_____
_____
_____
_____
_____

Do they each represent their respective company's message? How?

_____
_____
_____
_____
_____

List unique ways to express your brand message through a logo?

_____
_____
_____
_____
_____

What color combinations work for your style, identity and target market?

_____
_____
_____
_____
_____

BRANDING

List logo ideas that would unite you with your target market:

_____
_____
_____
_____
_____

Logo Sketches:

Build a tagline:

Who is your target market?

_____
_____
_____

What benefits do you provide them?

_____
_____
_____
_____

What is unique about your brand?

_____
_____
_____

How do you differ from the competition?

_____
_____
_____

What feelings do you hope to evoke in your consumers?

_____
_____
_____

What is the purpose of your brand/business?

_____
_____
_____

List possible taglines using the answers above:

_____
_____
_____
_____

BRANDING

_____
_____
_____

Use this space to sketch possible logo/tagline combinations

Networking:

List existing associations, organizations and clubs that you would be interested in joining:

_____
_____
_____
_____
_____
_____

List associations, organizations and clubs that you would consider creating:

_____
_____
_____
_____
_____
_____

For each organization that you've listed, ask yourself the following:

Does this organization represent both your target market and your brand? y/n

Are there opportunities within this group to create relationships with those in your target market? y/n

Does this organization's value fall in line with the values of your target market and yourself? y/n

Is this an organization that you can authentically enjoy being a part of? y/n

Are there possibilities for leadership positions within the organization? y/n

If you've answered yes to three or more of these questions, then the organization probably presents a great opportunity for developing relationships and generating referral business.

Advertising:

Annual Advertising and Marketing Budget: $_____

List possible Publications to advertise in:

_____
_____
_____
_____
_____
_____
_____
_____

For each publication ask yourself the following to evaluate the opportunity:

Is this publication reaching my targeted market on a regular basis?

Is my target market reading this publication?

How long do readers hang on to this publication before throwing out?

Is this publication reaching a broader range of demographics than necessary for success and therefore more expensive?

What is the cost of advertising Weekly/Monthly/Annually?

Can the publication work within my budget?

Does this publication fall in line with the values of my niche market?

What is the circulation, and how regularly do I need to advertise in this publication to be effective?

Direct Mail:

Before attempting to do anything with direct mail, you must first create your database. To determine which people to include in your database, answer the following questions:

List those in your sphere of influence:

_____
_____
_____
_____
_____
_____
_____
_____

What groups and organizations make up my niche market?

_____
_____
_____
_____
_____

Who are the influential people within my target market?

_____
_____
_____
_____
_____

To determine how to find names and contact information for your database, the following questions will help get you started:

What groups, clubs and associations are associated with my niche?

_____
_____
_____
_____
_____
_____

What organizations market to my target niche market?

_____
_____
_____
_____
_____
_____

What networking groups, clubs and associations do I already belong to that are relevant to my niche market?

_____
_____
_____
_____
_____
_____

If you have a geographical niche, your local Association of Realtors, Title Companies and tax records are all good resources for obtaining mailing lists. Club directories and Internet cross reference sites are also great places to find target data to get you started. A solid database is the lifeblood of every branded agent.

Internet Marketing:

Whether you already have a website or are just beginning to create one, this checklist will help you stay focused on the essentials needed to develop a website that produces results.

Do you have a website?   y/n

Can potential consumers easily find your site with a simple web search?   y/n

Do you generate leads from your website?   y/n

Is your website consistent with your Visual Brand Identity?   y/n

Does your website contain an easy to use listing search tool that is accessible from the home page?   y/n

Does your search results provide numerous photos of each listing?   y/n

Does your website offer a 'request more information' option that delivers leads immediately to you?   y/n

Is your website promoting your brand more than the company you work for?   y/n

Is your web address memorable?   y/n

An effective website has to represent your brand identity and style and must be easy to find. The best websites include all of the above and more. If you've answered 'no' to any of the above questions, work quickly to improve these basics first.

Public Relations:

Press Kit:
A well-designed Press kit can easily put you ahead of your competition. Use this guide as a reference to create a winning press kit. Remember to keep extra kits on hand, sometimes with the media last minute opportunities are the best.

Personal Photo – Include printed and digital copies of your high quality black and white *and* full color branded photo. Include at least two different shots, because as you get more publicity the press will need different photo options.

References – Provide a page of references and testimonials from clients and networking associates. Name dropping here is not taboo, so if you have some clients who are well-known and liked in the community, get their testimonial of your brand and services to use in your kit and on the web.

Press Release – Include a few non time-sensitive releases in the kit to compel the media to do a spotlight piece on you, the local market expert.

Articles and Newsletters – Insert articles you've written, your branded newsletter, a printout of your web site, your blog, and a few direct mail pieces. Recipients of your kit are used to the usual herd materials, so show them your brand is different and better.

Personal Brochure – Your personal brochure tells your brand story and conveys your brand message. It should therefore be the centerpiece of your kit. The quality of a Broker/Agent piece can be so impressive that the media will often pass your brochure around the office.

Previous Media Coverage – Add a list or include copies of articles in which you've been quoted, referenced, or spotlighted. Listing your past media coverage ensures the press that you have already been a trusted and reliable source to other journalists.

Speaking Topics – Create credibility by listing topics about which you are prepared to speak and provide brief descriptions of each.

FAQs – List common questions and answers that are relevant to your business and target niche. This makes the journalist's job easier by providing quick filler if they ever need it.

Personal Brochure:

Use the space below to begin crafting your personal brochure copy/bio. What is unique about you? What are you passionate about? Tell your story here:

_____
_____
_____
_____

Brand Commandments

Use this series of self assessment questions to reevaluate your brand, or for guidance anytime you need reassurance or reinforcement:

Consistency

- Does your brand represent a consistent brand message through each of the 7 Brand Channels?
- Is your look and style consistent in all of your marketing and advertising?
- Are your brand standards consistent in everything that you do?
- Does everyone that works under your brand understand the standards and vision of your brand?
- Is the feedback that you receive and the perception of your brand consistent with the brand that your are trying to be?

Quality

- Do you exemplify the quality upon which your brand should be built?
- Do your clients experience the quality that your brand promises?
- Are you doing all the little things to ensure quality in every component of your real estate business?
- Are your marketing and advertising pieces of the quality that is expected of your brand?

Authenticity

- Are you remaining true to your self in all aspects of the three steps and in each of the 7 components?
- Does your brand continue to be relevant and to benefit the target niche that you serve?

- Is your brand still aligned with your passion?
- Is the life that you are living in line with the perception of your brand?
- Do you genuinely enjoy your every day working your brand and serving your target market?
- Are you living the life that you were meant to live?
- Are you maintaining balance between your business, your health and the people you love?

Accessibility

- Are you mentally and physically available to serve your target market?
- Are you committed to continually live in and interact with your target market?
- Are you the same brand that you were when you first succeeded?
- Are you doing the little things that make your brand different and special to your target market?

Reinvesting

- Are you continuing to reinvest in your brand?
- Are you consistently putting at least 15% of your income back into exposing your brand?
- Are you adjusting your reinvestment as your income grows?

- Do you continually seek better branding methods while maintaining consistency of your exposure?
- Are you reinvesting the energy that you get from your brand's success back into your target market?

Branded Agent Resources

Branding:

www.brandedcow.com

- *U R a Brand! How Smart People Brand Themselves for Business Success* by Catherine Kaputa
- *The Brand Called You: The Ultimate Personal Branding Handbook to Transform Anyone into an Indispensable Brand* by Peter Montoya and Tim Vandehey
- *Be Your Own Brand: A Breakthrough Formula for Standing Out from the Crowd* by David McNally and Karl D Speak
- *Building Strong Brands* by David A. Aaker

Specialization:

- *The 80/20 Principle: The Secret to Success by Achieving More with Less*
- by Richard Koch
- *The E-Myth Revisited : Why Most Small Businesses Don't Work and What to Do About It* by Michael E. Gerber

- *Differentiate or Die: Survival in Our Era of Killer Competition* by Jack Trout, Steve Rivkin

Style and Identity:

www.e-agent.biz/Realtors

- *Logo Design Workbook: A Hands-On Guide to Creating Logos* by Noreen Morioka, Terry Stone Sean Adams
- *Design Matters: Logos 01: An Essential Primer for Today's Competitive Market* by Capsule
- *Color Smart: How to Use Color to Enhance Your Business and Personal Life* by Mimi Cooper and Arlene Modica Matthews
- *Influence: The Psychology of Persuasion* by Robert B. Cialdini

Internet:

Web sites:

www.realestatewebmasters.com/
www.alamode.com
http://www.agentimage.com

SEO:

www.google.com/webmasters
http://help.yahoo.com/l/us/yahoo/search/basics/

- *Search Engine Optimization For Dummies, Second Edition* by Peter Kent

Blogging:

www.realestatetomato.com
www.brandidentityguru.com

- *The Rough Guide to Blogging 1* by Rough Guides
- *Clear Blogging: How People Blogging Are Changing the World and How You Can Join Them* by Bob Walsh
- *Blogging for Business: Everything You Need to Know and Why You Should Care* by Shel Holtz and Ted Demopoulos

Web 2.0:

- *Unleashing Web 2.0: From Concepts to Creativity* by Gottfried Vossen, Stephan Hagemann

Email:

- *The Bliss or "Diss" Connection?: Email Etiquette for the Business Professional* by Cherie Kerr and Jim Doody

Social networking:

www.linkedin.com
www.facebook.com
www.myspace.com

- o *I'm on LinkedIn — Now What???: A Guide to Getting the Most OUT of LinkedIn* by Jason Alba
- o *Plug Your Business! Marketing on MySpace, YouTube, blogs and podcasts and other Web 2.0 social networks* by Steve Weber

Networking:

- o *Dig Your Well Before You're Thirsty: The Only Networking Book You'll Ever Need* by Harvey Mackay
- o *Never Eat Alone: And Other Secrets to Success, One Relationship at a Time* by Keith Ferrazzi, Tahl Raz
- o *The Networking Survival Guide: Get the Success You Want By Tapping Into the People You Know* by Diane Darling
- o *Little Black Book of Connections: 6.5 Assets for Networking Your Way to Rich Relationships* by Jeffrey Gitomer
- o *Ten Commitments of Networking: Creative Ways to Maximize Your Personal Connections* by Larry James
- o *The Little Book of Big Networking Ideas* by Nadia Bilchik

Newsletters:

www.constantcontact.com
www.emailbrain.com

Direct Mail:

http://www.merrillcorp.com
http://www.xpressdocs.com/

- ***Direct Mail Pal: A Direct Mail Production Handbook*** by Ken Boone, Terry Woods, John Leonard, T. J. Tedesco
- ***Sold!: Direct Marketing for the Real Estate Pro*** by Lois K. Geller

Advertising:

- ***Creative Advertising: Ideas and Techniques from the World's Best Campaigns*** by Mario Pricken
- ***Made You Look: How Advertising Works and Why You Should Know*** by Shari Graydon
- ***Made to Stick: Why Some Ideas Survive and Others Die*** by Chip Heath and Dan Heath
- ***Ogilvy on Advertising*** by David Ogilvy
- ***Positioning: The Battle for Your Mind*** by Al Ries, Jack Trout
- ***Romancing the Brand: The Power of Advertising and How to Use It*** by David N. Martin
- ***Consumer Behavior (8th Edition)*** by Michael Solomon

Public Relations:

- ***The New Rules of Marketing and PR: How to Use News Releases, Blogs, Podcasting, Viral Marketing and Online Media to Reach Buyers Directly*** by David Meerman Scott
- ***Complete Publicity Plans: How to Create Publicity That Will Spark Media Exposure and Excitement*** by Sandra L. Beckwith
- ***Full Frontal PR: Building Buzz About Your Business, Your Product, or You*** by Richard Laermer

Personal Brochures:

Broker Agent Magazine: http://www.gotobam.com/
Hobbs Herder: www.hobbsherder.com

- ***The Marketing Power of Emotion*** by John O'Shaughnessy, Nicholas Jackson O'Shaughnessy
- ***May I Have Your Attention, Please: Build a Better Business by Telling Your True Story*** by Chris Hilicki and Andy Andrews

Customer Service:

- ***Branded Customer Service: The New Competitive Edge*** by Janelle Barlow and Paul Stewart
- ***Superior Customer Service: How to Keep Customers Racing Back to Your Business–Time Tested Examples from Leading Companies*** by Dan W. Blacharski

- *Super Service: Seven Keys to Delivering Great Customer Service...Even When You Don't Feel Like It!...Even When They Don't Deserve It!* by Jeff Gee and Val Gee
- *Exceptional Customer Service: Going Beyond Your Good Service to Exceed the Customer's Expectation* by Lisa Ford, David McNair, and Bill Perry

Life Balance:

- *The Balancing Act: Mastering the Five Elements of Success in Life, Relationships, and Work* by Sharon Seivert
- *Life Is Not Work, Work Is Not Life: Simple Reminders for Finding Balance in a 24/7 World* by Robert K. Johnston, J. Walker Smith

Realtor Resources:

NAR: www.realtor.org
Broker Agent Magazine: www.gotobam.com

BRANDED AGENT RESOURCES

Learn more about Personalized Real Estate Branding

Branded Cow
Real Estate Branding

Visit www.BrandedCow.com for more information on discovering, building, and becoming your brand. Featuring insightful information and resources including:

- Branded Boot Camps – Half day, full day and weekend hands on workshops are available, register today!
- Branded E- Newsletters
- Customized One-on-One Coaching
- "Brand in a Box" Branding System featuring personalized logo, tagline and customizable ad templates that are made specifically for you!
- Books
- Networking
- Blogs
- Audio CD's
- Branding Assessment Tests
- Networking
- Branded Agent Case Studies
- Branded Inner Circle Tele-conferences
- Useful Downloads, Tips, Resources and much more!

Please direct email inquires to: Amy@BrandedCow.com

About the Authors

Mark Hughes and Amy Young founded Branded Cow Marketing LLC after spending several years in the real estate industry and realizing that their seemingly obvious branding system had afforded them the luxury of becoming a top agent team simply through their branding expertise and relationships that followed. Designed and led by Mark, the team consistently ranked in the top 1% of Realtor teams nationwide and produced well over half a million dollars a year in income. As more and more opportunities arose such as an opportunity to speak at the RE/MAX National Convention and a guest spot on HGTV's National Open House, Mark and Amy realized that the personal branding process that was second nature to them; clearly was not as obvious to their competitors. After being approached by countless agents asking for help and advice on growing their business, Mark and Amy decided to develop their personal branding approach into a streamlined system that continues to help other agents achieve great success while maintaining balanced lives.

Mark Hughes

Mark Hughes is the President of Branded Cow Marketing LLC, a real estate branding company that consults with and educates Realtors on how to differentiate and become top performers. He has consistently been ranked in the top 1% of real estate agents worldwide, and is currently broker and owner of luxury real estate company BFP Sotheby's International Realty in Delaware. Mark is a graduate of the University of Virginia and has a diverse range of experiences in the real estate industry which have included mortgage company vice president, licensed real estate instructor, and residential developer. Mark has been featured on HGTV's National Open House and currently conducts workshops across the nation that educate Realtors on how to achieve their personal and business goals. Mark currently resides in Pennsylvania with his wife Judy and two children.

Amy Young

Amy Young is the Vice President of Branded Cow Marketing LLC. a real estate branding company dedicated to helping Realtors develop and maintain a long-term top performing brand. Amy spent several years as an award winning real estate agent for RE/MAX and SKY Sotheby's on the west coast of Florida. Before beginning her Real Estate and consulting career, Amy's experiences included Marketing and business development for several fortune 500 companies including L'Oreal, USA and the Pepsi Bottling Group. Amy graduated from Western Michigan University with a B.B.A in Marketing and currently resides in Connecticut with her husband, Jason.

Made in the USA
Lexington, KY
05 January 2010